ESSEX MAN GOES WILD
Notes on Nature

Essex Man Goes Wild

Notes on Nature

Bill Goldsmith

TABLE OF CONTENTS

List of illustrations

Foreword

This book was born of my retirement. It evolved from starting a nature journal a number of years ago and then, more recently, a series of short articles for inclusion in the Basildon Natural History Society's quarterly bulletin. At what point I decided that I would collect together my ramblings, I am not sure. Maybe it was after one or two kind comments on my jottings from family or members of the society that gave me the idea and the impetus.

Once the seed was sown and,having additional spare time, I started to record more of my experiences and observations with a book in mind. At the same time, the realisation of how little I knew about wildlife hit home but, rather than discourage me, I thought my book might just encourage others to look a little closer and find out more about mother nature's intricate web and, above all, to delight in it at any level.

I also wanted to show that living in an area such as South East Essex with its industry and population was not a barrier to enjoying wildlife. I wanted to share my experiences of finding the often mundane species surviving against a background of forever encroaching human demands. I would draw comfort from seeing wildlife living beside industrialisation. Finding a wasp spider astride its web, not five hundred yards from the fence of an oil refinery, or lizards sunning themselves on a flyover support, somehow elevates their existence.

Not that this book is solely about South East Essex. In fact, the majority is about elsewhere but I think that living in this crowded part of England gives me a heightened appreciation of the wilder parts of our countryside.

This book consists of a number of short (some very short) articles that describe, to the best of my limited ability and command of the English language, my observations, views, feelings and experiences of nature. Some articles are light-hearted and some heart-felt.

You will also notice that I am also no expert with the camera but I hope my photographs or the more professional efforts of my friend Ken Laban are at least descriptive and help explain some of the text. I must admit I now find the digital camera an important accessory on any field trip, mainly to take pictures in the hope of putting a name to the subject later. Then with growing confidence in using technology, I started to incorporate the digital pictures within the articles. I have always enjoyed painting and, once again, I apologise for the standard of the illustrations included in this book but they do help me recall certain sights, memories or experiences.

I would like to think that this book will encourage others with a limited knowledge to look a little closer at the natural world around them and, consequently, derive more enjoyment. No matter where you live, there is always something to watch and learn from. I would certainly recommend joining a local society to meet like-minded people and, perhaps more importantly, experts who can give you help and knowledge in most branches of natural history.

The interest that my wife and I have in nature also impacts on our eating and shopping habits, resulting in trips to farmers' markets, seeking out organic produce, carefully reading the country of origin on supermarket items and trying to buy British (food miles and animal welfare are other considerations) and, in some cases, boycotting products such as woodcock and hare or trying to buy wine sealed with cork stoppers. Shopping for us can be a slow process at times.

Gardening also means us sharing with nature; we do not use any insecticides or herbicides, we are not tidy (or it could be we are just lazy),we always leave a few apples and pears either on the tree or as windfall for wildlife and the hazelnuts are shared (albeit reluctantly at times) with both the grey squirrel and the great spotted woodpeckers. In a small way, we try to live with nature.

I must stress again that this is not a book based solely on scientific facts from reference books or the internet but usually thoughts or conclusions from my own observations or knowledge passed on to me from others who I would consider to be knowledgeable amateurs and the occasional professional. In some cases, if it sounds an absolute lie but it is interesting or might get a laugh - I might use it.

In other words, do not use this as a reference book if you want to pass an exam but I hope it will at least make you realise that you do not need to be an expert to enjoy the wildlife around you, wherever you may live.

Bill Goldsmith - 2014

Bird Notes from Thirty Years Ago
2006

Rummaging through an old notebook, I came across some scribbled observations on the ringed plover that I had made over a period of approximately four years in the 1970s. I am not sure how representative, or indeed how accurate the observations were, as they were made way back in what was then the Mobil Oil Refinery at Coryton in Essex and (being a shift worker at the time) they were often made during the hours of darkness when illuminated by floodlights. On the other hand, I believe this gave me an opportunity to witness some behaviour that perhaps was thought to happen only during the day.

During that period, ringed plovers nested in a number of locations throughout the refinery; on the shingled areas between the storage tanks or process units and probably totaled between 10-20 breeding pairs. The shingle was imported and laid over large areas of bare earth to make the place look smarter. The birds would choose the quieter and more open parts of the refinery where human disturbance was lower and vehicle movements minimal.

The birds would only be seen infrequently in the refinery between September and January but sightings tended to increase in February. In the last week of February or early March courtship would begin and took place during the night as well as in daylight. The male or sometimes two, with their bodies held low, heads outstretched, breast feathers puffed up and tail feathers fanned out, would make darting runs at the female. Mating also took place during darkness as well as daytime.

It is said that ringed plovers do not make a nest but make use of a suitable shallow depression in the ground and I must admit I have never seen a bird 'excavating' a nest site. However, I am sure that they did on occasion 'line' the depression with stones collected from elsewhere. I came to this conclusion after finding one or two nests where the small stones in the nest were distinctly uniform in size but different in size and colour from the stones surrounding the nest. They would often choose the areas that had smaller size shingle with gaps of bare or stony earth. The birds began sitting in early April and towards the end of the month the nests would usually contain four eggs. Talking to another refinery birdwatcher, we both believed that the plovers may 'mould' the nest depression as the four eggs always seemed to fit so neatly in the cup.

One of the numerous dangers facing ground nesting birds in the refinery was the bi-annual weed spraying which, as much as we tried to complete before the nesting period, would invariably be extended in some areas due to a delay or a problem. In these cases, we relied on individuals pointing out where the nesting birds were and then the sprayers leaving a suitable exclusion zone around the nest. It always pleased me that so many refinery workers took the welfare of the birds seriously. Indeed, I can remember planned work on an oil storage tank being postponed to later in the year due to a pair selecting a nest site within 3 feet of the tank. And then there is the obvious danger of the eggs being trodden on, which, to my horror, I once did in the fire training area.

Normally, the first indication of a nest is when you see the parent bird engaged in its diversion tactics to distract an intruder away from the eggs. Finding the well camouflaged nests without treading on them requires you to take part in the bird's ploy. Firstly, the parent quietly leaves the nest unseen and runs in a direction away from the nest and, when at a 'safe' distance, stops and calls loudly to draw your attention. Then, you need to walk towards the bird which then runs a little further away, stops, and repeats the bobbing and calling. Once again, you follow the bird and the whole sequence is repeated until the bird decides you have been lured far enough away from the nest to no longer be a threat. The bird then falls silent and flies in a large arc to land back near its nest and then, if satisfied all was well, you can watch it run swiftly back to the nest and resume incubating.

The tactics employed varied: some birds seemed more nervous than others as some would sit tight until you were within 30 feet of the nest, whereas others would move if you were within 200 feet. It also appeared that the number of eggs, or how close to hatching they were, had an influence on the bird's behaviour. The longer the birds have been incubating the eggs the more likely they were to sit tight or, when they did run, they would on occasion use the broken wing trick to try and draw you away from the nest. They did not appear to use this ploy if there were less than four eggs.

Although we would all try to minimise disturbance to the sitting birds, they would sometimes choose a nest site close to where we had to inspect or operate running equipment. In these cases, once we knew where the nest was, we would try to approach from a different direction and keep the time we spent in the area to a minimum.

One night, I witnessed a fox walking close to a nest and the bird gave a memorable broken wing performance to attract the fox away although I am not convinced it was the bird's antics that caused the fox to miss the nest as he barely altered his course. It just happened he was not going in that direction anyway! More likely he was heading for the canteen and roast chicken as the night shift were fond of feeding the foxes any leftovers.

As the eggs hatched around the end of April or early May, it was rare to find chicks and eggs in the nest at the same time. It appeared that as soon as the chick emerged it would leave the nest almost immediately. At some nests, the number of eggs would reduce each day until empty. I never saw any broken egg shell in the nest.

The chicks would later be seen feeding with the parents in the small pools of water that gathered in low lying areas, sometimes even beneath the rows of pipes. All the chicks appeared to be able to feed themselves very early on as I never witnessed them being fed but have seen them probing in the mud and vegetation around the pools. When the parent bird gave an alarm call the chicks would freeze or, now and then, drop on their fronts and the parents would, once again, try to lead the intruder away from where the chicks were located.

I am not sure but I think some pairs had two broods, as nests with eggs would be found up to the middle of June but it may be that their first nest failed or maybe they were just late. I am fairly confident that the majority of eggs hatched successfully because most nests would have four eggs and then the number of eggs would slowly reduce. If it was predation by crows, gulls or foxes, then I would think that all the eggs would have gone at once. One other point - most of the refinery birdwatchers agreed that they could not remember the same nest site being used either for a second brood or the following year.

Sadly, the numbers dwindled over the years and by 2005 we could not find any breeding pairs. The downturn would appear to follow local trends rather than a refinery issue.

It is only when I sat down to write this that I realised how many gaps and uncertainties there were in my notes but then again I was at work.

Snow Buntings in Southend
February 2006

My wife and I recently joined the ranks of computer owners and we are slowly starting to find our way around the Internet. Naturally, two of the first sites I chose to visit was the RSPB and the South East Essex RSPB Local Group. The latter gives you all the recent sightings in the area and I noticed that there had been regular reports of nine snow buntings on Southend seafront, east of the old gasworks. Having never seen this bird of the bare mountain tops, I decided to go on a 'twitch' (just a small one) and, despite it being a wet, windy and cold morning, I persuaded my wife to join me.

As we drove along the almost deserted seafront, I was looking for the presence of other birdwatchers to give us a clue as to the location of the birds. I know that's lazy but, as it happened, there were none around so we had to find them ourselves. We parked up, got out of the car and it felt very cold in the biting wind. We scanned the beach but, apart from a small flock of delightful sanderlings darting back and forth on whirling legs along the tide line and the odd turnstone sifting through the seaweed, there were no buntings to be seen. After about twenty minutes we retreated back to the comfort of the car but not to be thwarted we drove the half a mile back towards the Kursaal and tried again; this time I left my wife in the shelter of the car reading the paper while I continued the search. After another ten minutes or so of scanning, a flock of 'finch like' birds flew past slowly, being buffeted by the wind, which gave me the chance to count them; nine - I think! Surely it had to be them? They landed on the beach not far away and, after approaching slowly, keeping my eyes glued to the spot where they dropped, I was soon looking at my first snow buntings urgently feeding along the high tide line. After a while, I returned to the car for my wife but by the time we got back to the spot they had gone. We did relocate them further along the beach but my wife found it difficult to pick out these restless birds as they blended well with the bleached colours of the shore and in addition it had started to rain and that required us to keep clearing the lenses on the binoculars. The birds then flew off, so with frozen faces we headed back to the car and drove to Leigh-on-Sea and the warmth of the Crooked Billet for a drink followed by a visit to Osborne's to buy jellied eels, cockles, winkles and whelks to take home for lunch.

Whilst enjoying our seafood (with the central heating on). I could not help but reflect on those small, delicate buntings constantly searching for morsels on that cold, windswept shoreline but I suppose, compared to the winter conditions in their normal breeding grounds of mountain side and high tundra, Southend seafront is not too uncomfortable.

I know the light was bad and they were in winter plumage but even so they had less white on them than I expected, maybe due to images from my books of the males in summer plumage with their dazzling white bodies and black wings still lingering in my mind. The white showed better when they took to flight and their longish wings are quite noticeable on the ground.

I was grateful that someone else had made the information available, to enable me to watch and wonder at these winter visitors for the first time.

Snow Bunting on Shoebury Beach

On Rainham Marshes
February 2006

The RSPB were conducting tours of their newly opened reserve at Rainham Marshes and a friend and I decided to join one on Saturday in February, mainly due to the fact that penduline tits had been seen there earlier in the week. It was obvious that the news had spread as there were fifty or sixty expectant people present when the walk started.

We set off, following the warden like an army in a uniform of dull green, brown or blue clothing with matching headgear, our boots resonating on the boardwalks. Soon our attention was grabbed by two birdwatchers ahead of the main group who were waving at us and pointing to the reed beds. I assume that the vast majority of the group were birdwatchers, judging by the number of telescopes, cameras and binoculars present and that most had come to see the tits. Therefore, in response to the waving, the pace of the group instantly quickened and an excited rising murmur could be heard.

Sure enough,when we reached the spot, there were two penduline tits feeding on the seed heads of the reedmace and they were very close to the pathway. Thankfully, these birds were feeding obligingly on the seeds and paid no attention to us whatsoever, giving everybody excellent views of the birds. They even ignored a loud blast of the Eurostar train horn as it sped by along the adjacent railway line. I was pleased to see that some of those with telescopes in the best viewing places were allowing other birdwatchers to view the birds through their scopes, giving everyone an opportunity of a close up view of these rare little winter visitors and for me this vagrant was a 'lifer'.

Watching the bird watchers that day, I noticed that many of them were using digital cameras on their telescopes to photograph the birds.

You could see the tits busily pecking away at the seeds, pulling apart the head of the reedmace and, at times, they would be partly obscured by the clumps of fluffy down being dislodged. As the birds moved from one head to another, you could locate the birds by watching for the falling white seed heads, some drifting in the breeze. I was informed that the birds were in fact a male and female and the differences pointed out to me. The male is distinguished by a larger and more clearly defined black mask but both have a grey head, a chestnut back and are the size of a blue tit. Eventually the birds decided to feed elsewhere in the reed bed and were no longer in sight and so we left to catch up the main body of the group who had continued on the walk.

Further along there were areas of open shallow water which held shoveller, wigeon, mallard, teal and pintail. The male pintail must be one of the most handsome of ducks. The pools also held common, great black backed and black headed gulls. At one point a cloud of nervous birds took flight as a Peregrine falcon came swooping in but was unsuccessful mainly due to a carrion crow who decided to try and intercept and harry the falcon. Frustrated, the peregrine flew away and settled high on an electricity pylon beside the busy A13 road overlooking the marsh.

As we were lagging behind, watching a pair of stonechats, we could see that the main group had taken a slight detour to look at something. As they came back, we were informed that it was a black redstart. Lucky for us the bird was still there when we arrived, in full view on the top of a pile of road planings at the edge of the reserve and so we had an unexpected bonus for the day.

As the tour continued to the South of the reserve towards the river, a few of us decided to backtrack and see if the penduline tits had come back. We could see a small group of birdwatchers still at the same spot and, as we approached, they said there were now four birds. It turned out to be three females and one male and once again they gave a lovely exhibition. You could see that the birds had ripped most of the reedmace heads apart with the willowy down hanging in clumps or had drifted and caught on nearby reed stalks. We spent another fifteen minutes or so watching them feeding, then left to meet with the rest of the group in the car park.

I have only recently read that the birds are in fact searching for the caterpillars of tiny moths that live within the seed head, rather than actually eating the seeds themselves. In 2012 it was reported that not only penduline tits exploit this food source but also bearded tits, reed buntings, stonechats, blue tits, wrens and even a magpie was seen to exhibit this behaviour. Aren't birds clever!

Waxwings and Supermarket Car-Parks
March 2006

These days, the now regular appearance of waxwings (Bombycilla garrulus) in supermarket car parks is well-documented but I still feel I need to add my own experience. The particular supermarket in question is Aldi's in Pitsea which has a car park with berberis hedges laden with berries dividing the rows of parking spaces and, over a number of weeks this winter, a flock of up to forty two waxwings had been seen feeding hungrily on the yellow berries.

Now, supermarket car parks may not be the best places for the self-conscious birdwatcher peering through a pair of binoculars while shoppers are going about their business but you may strike it lucky -as I did on this occasion. I had parked towards the rear of the car park and within five to ten minutes the birds flew to a low tree in the next row to me. I was afforded great views from the comfort and relative anonymity of my van. I do admire those birdwatchers that set up their telescopes in busy public places and I am always pleased to 'join in' when others are already watching birds.

I don't think anybody can fail to appreciate the beauty of these starling sized birds, with a buff/light-brown body, grey rump and yellow and black on the wings. The handsome crest and the fact that they travel from Russia/Siberia and turn up in a concrete jungle just adds to the magic. In the field, I could also see a small spot near the wing tip (I have trouble in describing the colour but it seemed to be a pinky/cherry-red). Later when I looked up the bird in one of my books it explains that the waxwing gets its name from the red spot on the wing close to the tip which, on reflection, describes the colour perfectly - that of red sealing wax.

I tried to count the birds but each time one or two of them would change position in the tree or a starling would join them which was enough to put me off and I ended with counts in the region of thirty three to thirty eight. The birds would wait for a lull in the movement of shoppers and then swoop down en masse to a particular part of the hedge and greedily devour the berries. As the flock flew down and away from me, the yellow band at the tips of their tails showed brightly in the grey surroundings. After a few minutes feeding they would all fly back to the same nearby tree. I was not sure what triggered their return as there did not always appear to be people or cars approaching them. When in the tree, they all faced in the same direction.

While watching from my vehicle several people passed by the tree where the thirty or more birds were only twenty foot above them but they did not glance up or seem to notice. Perhaps they were regular shoppers and, after all, the birds had been there for some weeks (or maybe they thought they were starlings?)

It just goes to show that it is possible with some 'green planning' to give wildlife a helping hand even in a relatively inhospitable environment such as a car park.

I wonder if we will see them back next winter?

***

Oh but what a winter (2010/2011) turned out to be with a veritable invasion of waxwings, flocks of up to two hundred birds being reported in the cold and snowy conditions. And not only in supermarket car parks, I saw a small flock of around ten waxwings in the back gardens along my road in Corringham and then, to my utter delight, three of them landed in a tree in our garden! I never believed that this beautiful visitor would ever appear on my garden list! This was also the first time I had heard their delightful, high pitched, ringing call.

The high numbers in Pitsea eventually attracted the attention of a local sparrowhawk and after a couple of earlier reports of near misses, a waxwing was taken from a flock of around forty birds at the Aldi car-park. The sparrowhawk was obviously not discriminating on the grounds of rarity or miles travelled when it came to a meal! Another amazing report was on the 3/5/11 where a flock of twelve birds were still at Rayleigh Mount and a swift was flying overhead!

So far this winter (2011/2012) there have been reports of a single, lonely waxwing in Pitsea and, when we found it, it was consorting with a number of starlings - looking for company, no doubt!

Waxwings in Corringham

In Search of a Bird
April 2006

As a child I participated in that horrible schoolboy pastime of collecting wild birds' eggs and, armed with information from the *Observers' Book of Birds and Bird Eggs*, my friends and I would search the parks and open spaces in the East End of London for nests. We all had collections of eggs which were normally kept in an old drawer or box lined with sawdust with the eggs arranged in rows, usually starting with the largest at the top. Because of our age, our range was limited and,fortunately, so were the species whose eggs we stole. Sometimes we overcame this handicap by using our imaginations or stretching the truth and were able to turn a slightly differently marked egg of a common bird into one of a much rarer species. So that was how a blackbird's egg in my collection became an egg of a ring ouzel.

Maybe it was from this deception that I have always wanted to see a ring ouzel and over the years I have noted with envy the reports of birds being seen either on migration or at their somewhat remote breeding sites. I heard that this spring a female was seen in Gunners Park, Shoebury.

In Gilbert White's book "The Natural History of Selborne" he was trying to establish the migration pattern of this rather rare bird way back in 1767. He mentions eventually obtaining some specimens and notes that they were "juicy and well flavoured"! So even then the bird was not common. From what I have read recently the bird has continued to decline in numbers over the past   fifty years (not due to being eaten, I hope) and according to *Birds Britannica* just 8,300 pairs are present in England and Ireland.

So this April I managed to persuade three friends with whom I go walking to spend two days in the Derbyshire Dales in search of the ring ouzel (Turdus torquatus). Armed with information from a rock climber acquaintance (who also happens to be a birdwatcher), I was confident that this summer migrant could be seen at Stannage Edge, an impressive rocky outcrop famed amongst climbers. We set out from the village of Hathersage and walked for approximately three miles slowly gaining height until we reached the base of the Edge. The ridge runs for approximately two miles and we had arrived roughly in the middle where the rocks were at their highest and, within five minutes, a male ring ouzel hopped on to a huge rock that had fallen from the main face. We only saw it for about thirty seconds before it flew away but what a sight this 'blackbird' made, framed against the background of rocks, with its white crescent on the chest clearly visible.

We searched for the bird but were unable to relocate it; in fact we walked the whole length of the ridge without another confirmed sighting. I say confirmed because at one point our hopes were raised but it turned out to be just a blackbird. You would think that our common blackbird had enough habitats without infringing on ring ouzel space.

Tired, having covered around five miles, our route back was still another 4 miles and it included a high point called Higger Tor. As we approached the Tor we consulted the map and found we could take a short cut and avoid the walk to the top. Opinion was split but the fittest amongst us spoke those immortal words "no pain, no gain" and, not wishing to appear wimps, we all climbed to the top. I am so glad we did. Just before the peak we spotted a female ring ouzel and then, as she disappeared behind some rocks, a male was spotted only about fifty four foot away.

This male bird was very obliging and allowed us to get close. In addition to the distinctive white, crescent shaped breast band, we could see through binoculars the white edges to the flight feathers and the small white patch on the forewing. We managed to take a number of photographs and they are stunning, even showing the pale edges to the feathers on the flanks and breast which forms a faint pattern and the beak is yellow with a black/ brown tip. We slowly retreated and left the bird pecking around in the dead bracken, seemingly unconcerned at being a star turn.

About a mile on as we were descending we saw another 'blackbird' in a stunted bush and yes it was a male ring ouzel, proving they are not always in rocks. This bird had some extra flecks of white around the head.

It did concern me that the number of climbers and walkers, including some parties of twenty or more people, would create an unacceptable level of disturbance to the birds in this popular area. Happily, we did see some signs asking people not to use certain paths to reduce disturbance to nesting ring ouzels.

Back at the B&B with our feet up after a nine mile round trip we were tired but happy

As for me, I did feel a certain satisfaction at planning the trip and I will now hopefully move on to another bird that has always fascinated me since my schoolboy days but I have never seen -the hawfinch.

Male Ring Ouzel

Mediterranean Gull
April 2006

I never expected that the muddy Thames estuary at Southend-on-Sea in April would be the place to look for an exotically named gull but according to a friend they often turn up there.

Having checked the tide tables, we timed our visit to arrive a couple of hours before high tide, thinking that the incoming water would bring any birds closer. The morning was sunny but still felt cold in the light North East wind. Following directions from my friend, the two of us parked on the sea front between Rossi's and the Casino, crossed the road, set up our telescopes and began to scan the mudflats.

The mudflats stretched out before us and we could see waders such as oystercatcher, curlew, redshank and also nine brent geese all busily feeding. The gulls tended to gather in the pools of water but consisted of mainly black headed gulls with a sprinkling of common and herring but no sign of a mediterranean gull.

Looking through my binoculars I could see some 'lumps' on a distant mudbank which on closer inspection with the telescope turned out to be eight seals. I have heard of the odd seal being reported in the Thames but eight seemed a lot and one appeared to be a youngster as it was much smaller. Due to the distance I am not sure but I think they were Grey seals.   If anyone knows which and whether this a common sight, I would be interested to know.

Eventually the lure of Rossi's became too great and we just had to pop in for refreshments and to warm up. While drinking our coffee someone walked past outside armed with a fork and bucket and headed out on to the mudflats looking as if he was going bait digging - strange we thought as the tide should be up in an hour?

Outside, we continued our search for the elusive gull and as we gazed out over the mudflats which were by now more expansive than when we first arrived, it dawned on us that the tide was going out and I had read the tide table wrongly. It would in fact be low tide and not high tide in one hour, an easy mistake surely? On the positive side I did remember to add the hour on to compensate for BST...

Did we give up? No, we continued to scan the gulls and I contented myself with trying to differentiate between black headed gulls that had not developed the full hood and common gulls. As we watched, a flock of pigeons feeding nearby on the seafront attracted the attention of twenty to thirty gulls which circled and squawked above the pigeons. Having being briefed on the characteristics of the Mediterranean gull I noticed one gull which appeared whiter than the others and almost immediately my friend said: "that's it!" .Thankfully the birds stopped wheeling furiously and dispersed enabling us to follow the mediterranean gull with our binoculars as it landed on the mud not too far away. We took a short walk to one of the seafront benches, set up our telescopes and had a comfortable view of the bird and what's more, to our astonishment, it was joined by a second.

The two birds sat close to each other on the mud in the sunshine and started to preen themselves. Both birds were adults and in summer plumage. They are distinguished from black headed gulls by their black hoods, not brown, which reach onto the nape. Their wings are a pale grey with white primaries rather than black as on the black headed Gull and their bill is heavier and red in colour with a black tip. Just to highlight the distinctions a black headed gull obligingly moved into view alongside the mediterranean gulls.

The sexes are similar and these birds gave us the impression they were a pair as when one moved a short distance the other would quickly rejoin. It was early April, they are in summer plumage, could they be breeding? According to "Birds Britannica" by 2000 there were at least 90 breeding pairs at 28 sites ranging from Kent to Cumbria, so it seems possible.

I find gulls very difficult to identify especially with juvenile, 1st, 2nd winters, adult, summer and winter phases to take into account, if fact I most often give up and lump them altogether. But it just goes to show that with some effort and encouragement you never know what you may turn up amongst those 'gulls'.

One obvious tip, but one we forgot, is to take a few slices of bread to bring the gulls closer and of course, get the tides right. With regard to the error on tides, on further investigation I found that I had looked at the 2005 tide table and not 2006 so I blame the Port of London Authority - fancy leaving 2005 tides on their website!

Mediterranean Gull in winter plumage

Passing Through Essex
August 2006

One of nature's wonders must be migration, especially of birds, some so small yet capable of covering massive distances and facing numerous dangers. Whilst the Swallow and Swift are among the well known exponents of this phenomenon, other small passerines can pass through our county virtually unheralded. One bird in particular that I feel is often missed and is a favourite of mine is the whinchat. Maybe this is because the bird does not breed in our area and can only been seen for rather brief periods when moving through, to or from, its breeding grounds in northern or western parts of the UK and, of course, they are not that common.

Mid August to mid September seems to be the best time to find these birds and the Fobbing marshes appear to be one of their South Essex stopping off points on their migration South (but never it seems, in the Springtime, or perhaps I just miss them?). With this in mind a friend and I set off along Marsh Lane in Fobbing, past fields of stubble and down onto the flat, open, mainly grassland of the marshes.

Apart from a few pigeons hurtling from cover and a dozen seagulls in the middle of a field we hardly saw or heard any other birds for over an hour but as usual in nature there is always something else to see and admire. At this point on a warm day it was dragonflies and butterflies that provided the main interest and although we could not identify many of them it did not stop our enjoyment. Then we saw a butterfly that we could immediately recognise - a clouded yellow, unmistakable with its black edged deep yellow, almost orange wings. Who needs birds?

As we continued walking along the edge of a wide meadow in the sunshine and silence, with nothing but a pair of blue tits added to our tally, we decided to scan the fence on the opposite side and could make out around four small birds on the barbed wire. Even with telescopes we could not identify them with certainty due to the distance and the heat haze but they did look like whinchats and behaved like whinchats by making periodic swoops for insects into the long dry, almost white grass and then flying back on to the wire or posts. We moved nearer and could now see that three of the birds were whinchats and the fourth was a wheatear, another bird just passing through on its way to its winter quarters. The Wheatear flew a short distance into the meadow showing its distinctive white rump and then disappeared from view, leaving just the whinchats. We advanced again and through the telescopes we could now fully appreciate these elegant, upright little birds with their warm orange-buff breast and streaky brown back. The birds were either females or juveniles both of which have a distinctive white/cream supercilium above a dark eye stripe but lack the small white patch at the front of the wing and the much darker facial pattern of the male.

What I love about 'chats' is that they perch in prominent positions and allow the observer the luxury of time to view them and, to show our appreciation, we walked away in a wide arc trying not to disturb their 're-fuelling'. Although we scanned a number of other similar fence-lines alongside rough grass no further birds were found, was there something special about that one?

Although we were very pleased to see the migrants it was disappointing that we never saw a reed bunting, yellow hammer, Linnet or a corn bunting, resident birds which you would expect to see in this habitat. Perhaps it was just one of those days!

A corn bunting on Fobbing Marsh

Red in Tooth and Claw
August 2006

I was sitting at the kitchen table, having just finished lunch when a movement in the garden through the glass back door caught my eye. It was a female sparrowhawk on the lawn about twenty yards away and I could see it had a male blackbird pinned to the ground by its talons. The movement that had caught my attention was the hawk giving a series of quick short flaps of its wings. Whether the bird was trying to improve its balance, or to get a firmer grip on her victim that was not quite dead, I was not sure. In those few seconds I wrestled with my conscience, should I open the door and scare off the killer or sit and watch what happens next? I remained seated, no further fluttering occurred and the hawk contented itself with looking in all directions to make sure she would not be disturbed. Another decision needed to be made - should I risk getting my binoculars and perhaps disrupt the bird's lunch? Did I even want a close up view of what might happen next? I couldn't resist; I went into the dining room and retrieved my binoculars.

Looking through the dining room windows I could see the bird's bright yellow eye giving it a fearsome gaze as it looked around for any signs of danger. With its strong yellow legs and talons keeping a firm grip on the victim it began to pluck clumps of feathers from the still body with its hooked beak; each time it stripped some feathers it would look up and glance around to make sure all was well. At this point my wife came into the room but did not take too much notice of me looking through binoculars, but I was faced with another decision – should I tell her what was unfolding in our back garden? Being a 'softy' she might run out and try to save the blackbird -after all this is the woman that averts her eyes at road kills and asks me not to point out any such bundles of fur or feathers and certainly not to identify the corpse...

I remained silent and continued to watch. Now the bird is tearing at the flesh and I could see a large piece of bright red meat in its beak which it promptly gulped down. While it was eating, the bird would move position and I was able to see the fine brown barring across the chest which continued down onto the thighs and also the pale stripe running above the large eye. I started to think - was this the same male blackbird that was trying to build a nest with its mate in our ivy only a month ago? Was it the same bird that I had seen 'anting' on the lawn in almost the same spot with its wings held slightly out, feathers puffed up, its head held slightly upwards and its beak open? My feelings of regret over not trying to scare the hawk off were then interrupted as my wife went out of the kitchen back door to the garage and the hawk flew off low over the hedge with its half-eaten meal still firmly gripped in its claws. On the lawn, all that was left of the drama was a scattering of feathers, some with tiny scraps of skin and flesh that the flies had already found.

A few hours later I went back out into the garden and disturbed a female blackbird on the lawn and as she ran away she passed by the feathers and once again I felt sadness at the thought it might have been her mate.

I have to tell myself that it is Nature's way of balancing biodiversity and I should not interfere but then I think: am I already interfering by feeding the birds and trying to make the garden wildlife friendly? Had I have stepped in, would the outcome have then been a hungry sparrowhawk and a badly injured blackbird?

Bill Goldsmith

I am not sure what my wife will say if she reads this but I am fairly certain that, if she does, then the next time she sees me peering through my binoculars she will ask me what I am looking at.

Birds: What Are We Doing?
September 2006

I do have misgivings about feeding birds. Whilst watching the sparrows feeding on peanuts from the feeder in my garden I could not help but notice that the weight of peanuts far outweighed the three birds by at least twenty times. Imagine yourself and a couple of friends trying to munch your way through a pie much heavier than yourselves? Also, this was on a warm day with plenty of healthy insects and ripe berries packed with roughage just waiting to be snapped up by an alert and agile bird but, no, the preference always seems to be the hi-protein giant ready meal in a basket.

Well, at least I make them peck away at the whole peanut to break off pieces which must be better than feeding them sunflower seeds which after a quick flip of the beak to remove the husk is virtually swallowed whole. Then of course there is the ultimate fast food for birds – premium sunflower hearts, no husks, just eat. Looking at the menu (or should I say the RSPB's catalogue), there is a whole range of foods for the not so energetic bird. For instance, dried mealworms: I mean, they are not even wriggling and require no digging, poking about in crevices or probing around in mucky soil to extract them and the bird requires no expertise to find them, except needing to know where the nearest RSPB member's bird table is sited.

Then there is bird cake; admittedly they do contain chopped up peanuts, cereals and either insects or berries but then they are in-cased in fat! What does that do to their arteries? To think that the generation of birds I am now feeding-and I have started to feed them all year round-will most likely not try too hard searching for their own food, knowing that there is a ready source of convenience food in various containers hanging from shrubs and trees in my garden. These same birds have bred nearby and are now bringing their offspring to these food rich havens without, I wouldn't mind betting, giving them any grounding in the art of recognising, finding, catching and eating of wild, free range, organic food. To make matters worse, I now put out water for them to drink and bathe in. I change it each day to ensure it is fresh, and it is not far from the feeders so there is now very little flying involved in between eating, drinking and perching whilst digesting. What did they do before? In dry periods they must have known where to find water and after rain would most likely find a nice clean puddle that might last them for days. Just how they are going to cope when I am on holiday - I am not sure?

I think we are in danger of producing future generations of overweight garden birds, with higher instances of diabetes and heart problems. Already you can see groups of plump youngsters hanging around the feeders looking disinterested, with nothing to do and leaving their empty food husks strewn on the ground.

Within the next ten years, I think that our garden birds will have all but lost their natural instincts for living off the land and be almost totally reliant on handouts from us. It may happen that a few 'wild' relatives, living in the more remote parts of the country, will retain the 'knowledge' and be able to pass it on to some of the future urban generation and so keep the traditional eating habits alive. Let's hope so.

I was going to go on and mention my provision of housing for the birds but I think I'll leave that for another day.

Scanning the internet for the effects of humans feeding birds was not too successful, with many comments on the need for more detailed scientific studies. On the negative side, what was clear was the possibility of an increased risk of disease transmission and predation by cats or raptors due to the higher than normal concentrations of birds. Therefore, good hygiene of both feeders and the surrounding areas is important so regular cleaning and moving of the feeders is a necessity, as is the sighting of feeders i.e. clear of undergrowth where cats can hide but near to cover should danger approach.

Less clear was the impact of birds whose condition may be artificially boosted by winter feeding and may therefore come into breeding condition too early but conversely may have more successful broods. In addition the behaviour and movements of birds may also be affected.

Both the RSPB and the BTO very much advocate the feeding of birds with the BTO stating there is scientific evidence highlighting the positive effects of supplementary food can have on birds e.g. it has been shown to improve overwinter survival rates for a number of species.

In any case I read that Chris Packham has a garden packed with bird feeders so if it is OK by him then it must be OK!

A sketch of my birdfeeder

A Useful Leylandii?
November 2006

Of all trees, the Leylandii probably suffers the most from a bad press. Often planted in rows along the boundaries of gardens, they can cut out sunlight and present a rather monotonous outlook/view and are the cause of many a dispute between neighbours. However, they can be of benefit to wildlife.

My neighbour has a single Leylandii roughly halfway down his garden and up against our boundary. The tree must be around 10 metres tall and at the very top it has split into two slender forks which are bent over and make an excellent pair of perches. Being among the tallest trees overlooking a number of gardens, I am sure this is one of the most sought after positions in the neighbourhood as, invariably, a bird or birds are seen occupying this lofty location. Quite often, I have seen progressively larger birds scatter smaller ones for the right to perch, usually ending up with a pair of collared doves or occasionally magpies in possession. It is also a favoured singing post for dunnocks, robins and blackbirds and even an occasional wren but, once again, it is not unusual to see the birds dispossessed even in mid-song. Mainly, during the winter months, it also becomes an occasional vantage point for a huge grey heron as it majestically surveys the surrounding garden ponds for signs of a meal. Needless to say, the heron with its dagger-like bill is rarely challenged for the right to perch except, that is, when the local pair of carrion crows take issue with his proximity to their patch! On these encounters the crows repeatedly swoop down, calling loudly, while the heron crouches, raises its crest and breast feathers and opens its dangerous looking beak in the direction of the assailants. Sometimes the heron decides it has had enough and flies away with slow beats of its large, broad wings; sometimes it stands it ground and the crows give up!

On more than one occasion, during fairly heavy rain with little wind and the rain almost falling vertically, I have watched two collared doves in residence at the top of the tree each fully stretch out a wing upwards and slowly lean over such that the rain was hitting the underside of their wings. After a minute or so they would both lean back, retract the wing and then lean the other way and stretch out the other wing. This sequence was repeated two or three times and I am sure I was witnessing synchronised showering. Yet another use for this exposed, versatile perch.

Being coniferous it also affords protection during the winter and most of the few sightings of goldcrests in the garden have been in the Leylandii; this, the smallest bird in Europe, quickly working through the branches searching for insects. But perhaps the most unusual bird to use the tree was a barn owl that was perched on the top one winter's evening in 2012.

In addition, my neighbour has attached two nestboxes to the trunk which have been used by great tits and house sparrows so all things considered it is not all bad news for this much maligned conifer!

Work Party – Baa?
December 2006

I have been on a number of conservation work parties over the years but I never thought one would involve rounding up sheep. So you can imagine my surprise when I turned up for an Essex Wildlife Trust work party and was told we were going to move some sheep.

On the Langdon Hills Reserve, Shetland breed sheep are used to manage the sward of the meadows by moving them from field to field over a period of years. Rotation ensures there are always areas of longer grass as well as short which help provide differing habitats for a wider range of invertebrates and plants. They are Nature's lawn mowers.

Two wardens, three other volunteers and I set out from the visitors centre in the Land Rover towing a trailer and a tractor fitted with a grass cutter. When we arrived at the field the ten sheep were quietly feeding at the bottom of a sloping field and barely gave us a glance as we piled out of the vehicles. So far so good, six men against ten sheep (not even fully grown, but this year's lambs) -it should be no problem! I should have perhaps taken into account that the night before had been very windy with the rain lashing down for a couple of hours in the early morning. Therefore, with a soggy, sloping field, patches of long grass and tangles of weeds, it should have raised some doubts in my mind.

The plan of action was outlined to us by the warden. First, the current to the electric fence surrounding the field was isolated and then we quickly put together a number of sections of aluminium framework to form a small pen just inside the outer fencing. Next, we erected more of the same electric fencing (but disconnected) running from the entrance of the pen and down the field for approximately fifty metres, forming a funnel with one side of the field's outer fencing, for us to herd the sheep along and into the pen. Then, once we had the sheep within the funnel we were to close the mouth of the funnel by moving the fencing to meet the outer fence. By now, the sheep were watching us!

We fanned out and walked slowly downhill on the right hand side of the field to get behind the sheep and then we turned with outstretched arms and walked in unison back up the field driving the sheep before us up the left hand side of the field. We managed to walk them into the open 'mouth' of the fence funnel but halfway towards the pen they sensed a trap, bolted sideways and then, to my amazement, the flock leapt as one at the four foot foot fence. Unfortunately the lead sheep did not quite clear the fence and caught the top, somersaulted and pulled the fence over allowing all the others to jump the leaning fence. All ten of them hurtled back past us and down the field, our boots were no match for their hooves, as the sheep nimbly sidestepped our inelegant lunges and slips in trying to stop them.

The sheep had returned to the bottom of the field and as they stood close together, heads pointing our way, we repeated the process. This time we herded them even closer to the pen but once again, at the last moment, they bolted and once again leapt the funnel fence at various points. Amazingly, one jumped straight into the arms of a warden but the rest escaped to the far end of the field. The next drive was much more successful and resulted in seven of them being herded along the funnel and shut in the pen. From the pen they were manually transferred to the trailer ready for transportation to their new home. That left just two at large and once more we started to herd the pair towards the pen and, once again, just as they were close to the entrance of the pen, they turned and this time headed full pelt straight for my section of the fence. Almost together, the sheep hit the fence to my right and I dived at the animals. When I looked up I had them both - alright, one was caught in the fencing- but I kept a hold of them until the others arrived and they bodily lifted them and carried them to the trailer. I got to my feet muddied but feeling pleased with myself.

Finally, with all the sheep safely in the trailer we could start to take down the fencing ready to be erected in their new field. As we worked, we could hear the rumblings of an approaching storm and towards the south west the sky was turning black. Forked lightning started to flash in the nearby hills - we worked faster but then the wind increased and the rain started, quickly turning to hail, as we ran for the shelter of the Land Rover.

The storm passed and with all the fence loaded it was only a short drive to the new field. The grass cutter was used around the perimeter to ensure that the fence had a clear base. Thankfully this was a much smaller field and it did not take us long to erect the fence. The sheep, rather perversely, took some persuading to leave the trailer but eventually they all trotted out as one into their new environment and in a short while were contentedly nibbling away at the grass at the far end of the field. We drove the Land Rover and trailer out of the field and completed the fencing. All that was left was for us was to replace their water trough and refill it with fresh water. Once we were all clear and the warning signs were in place, the fence was electrified.

As I reflected on the morning, I realised how far from the urban sprawl you feel in the reserve and no doubt being involved in handling sheep and out in a storm helped to reinforce this sentiment. Also, I had learned about sheep i.e. they are fast and can jump. I think it was about this time I started to feel the tingling sensation down one side of my face and realised that, in my headlong lunge at the sheep, I had put my face into a patch of stinging nettles.

Has Spring Sprung?
March 2007

From my house in Corringham it is only a five minute walk to the footpath at the bottom of White Lion Hill in Fobbing. The footpath, although overgrown in places with bramble and hawthorn, takes you through a small wooded area, then into more open ground with scattered bushes and beyond that you are looking out across the Fobbing marshes. Therefore, you can often find a variety of wildlife and this day was not an exception.

I set out with a friend to walk the route, armed with a telescope, binoculars, digital camera, mobile phone and notebook. I wondered whether I had over-equipped for a stroll down to the marsh.

We soon heard a chiffchaff calling from near the top of some tall trees which were still not in leaf and therefore the bird could be seen but no such luck in locating the mocking call of the green woodpecker. greenfinch, blue and great tits flitted from bush to bush and, high overhead, a sparrowhawk was circling in the sky. We noticed that the bird had a primary feather missing and, to help us decide whether it was a male or female, it was joined by a second, smaller, therefore male sparrow-hawk. The two engaged in what I would describe as 'aerial sparring', twisting and tumbling for a few minutes before going their separate ways.

Walking out onto the grazing marsh, we were treated to the 'trilling' song flight of the skylark, high in the blue cloudless sky. Then, in the distance, we spotted another resident of these open spaces; two hares were facing each other and, to our delight, rose on their hind legs and started 'boxing'. This was the first time I had witnessed this habit of the so-called "mad March hare" and we watched fascinated as the bouts of 'boxing' were interspersed with chasing around in tight circles and occasionally one individual would crouch and flatten its enormous ears. I was glad I had carried the telescope.

By now we had been out for a couple of hours and decided it was time for lunch so we walked back to the Iron Latch footpath and across to the Manorway road where we each enjoyed a magnificent bacon baguette from the mobile cafe.

Despite the industrial surroundings and the road tankers pounding past the eatery, close by is a good location for a glimpse of a lizard. Fly tipped hardcore and earth has been banked up to form a barrier for the cycle path and the grass and other vegetation has now grown up around it. The large chunks of concrete and bits of wood seem to provide an ideal spot for a lizard to sun itself and the surrounding vegetation is perfect for diving into at any sign of danger. On two occasions I had managed only the briefest of glimpses of the creatures before they darted for cover.

As we headed back, the afternoon temperature was a warm sixteen degrees with a light easterly wind and, therefore, we should not have been surprised at the number of butterflies about. Even so, I was impressed with our list which included peacock, comma, speckled wood and small tortoiseshell.

Our walk yielded mammals, reptiles, birds, butterflies and, if I could be certain of identification, I would include the flora but - the highlight of the day was the bacon roll (my wife keeps feeding me salads and other healthy foods!).

The snack-bar van!

The Dave Moore Hide
August 2007

A friend and I decided to spend some time birdwatching with another visit to our local 'patch', Fobbing Marsh. I call it birdwatching rather than the more modern term of 'birding' as the latter seems more frenetic and implies a certain level of skill which I think I do not possess and seems to suggest that you find interesting birds. On the other hand, birdwatching seems to me to be at a gentler pace, often seeing only the commoner birds and you are frequently left wondering what you did see.

At the start of the footpath we bumped into John Cook who farms a good part of the Fobbing Marsh with beef cattle. He is over 70 years of age, thick set, weatherbeaten as you would expect and has the 'twang' of an old Essex accent. As usual with John you have to spend some time chatting and he always has a story, quips and jokes to tell along with the usual moans about bureaucracy in farming but he does welcome birdwatchers who he considers do a service in keeping an eye on his land and stock.

As we take our usual route across the grazing marsh we can see three hares ahead of us, two crouch down in the grass but we can still see the black and white on their ears, the third one is on its haunches looking directly at us. As we continue along our route two of the hares bound away to a safe distance the third decides to stay put and even appears to lower its ears to avoid detection in the grass. Closer still, the hare finally decides we are too near and dashes away to join the others, its orange/brown fur and black and white tail clearly visible.

Ripening berries

Overhead, two sparrowhawks circle high in the blue sky. A single house martin was flying south.

The shrubs we pass are laden with blackberries, elderberries, haws and hips and together with teasels, numerous grasshoppers and plenty of other insects, a veritable feast you would have thought for a whole host of birds. Yet, apart from one or two Whitethroats is was strangely devoid of them.

By the time we reach the seawall around Holehaven Creek we have only added two curlews to our list. Peering over the top of the seawall we see an expanse of saltmarsh and beyond that the creek but even here it was, apart from numerous gulls, 'quite'. We proceed along in the lee of the wall and it is now quite hot and the flies and mosquitoes are beginning to bite which tended to hasten our footsteps towards the scrape. As we approach, despite the insect assault, we have to slow our pace in order not to disturb the birds. From a distance, we can make out a number of green sandpipers, a single ruff and lots of teal and lapwing but unfortunately we, or something, spooks the birds and they lift off as one and fly towards the creek so we take this opportunity to make for the hide on the edge of the scrape.

At the northern edge of the scrape there is a 'hut' with a sign saying 'The Dave Moore Hide'. Who is or who was Dave Moore I have no idea but the hide has been there for a number of years and in that time has undergone a series of upgrades. It is comfortable enough for two but any more and I think it would feel rather cramped. Inside it has a homely feel maybe because of the patterned carpet used to cover the seats. It has a viewing window over the scrape and another to the grassland to the rear. It is equipped with a small library of bird books, wall charts of the birds you are likely to see,

The Dave Moore Hide

a small pair of binoculars and of course the 'sightings' log book. The hide is not locked and we wonder how it has avoided vandalism and we can only think that your average vandal cannot be bothered to walk the distance involved and can find enough nearer targets for their gratification.

With the windows open and our telescopes set up we await the return of the birds and, sure enough, after about ten minutes and a reconnaissance circuit of the scrape, the birds start to land. To our delight, the green sandpipers return and then amongst them we notice one is much slimmer with a finer bill, less white underneath and darker wings; it is a wood sandpiper. Having two species of 'bobbing' sandpipers side by side gave us the opportunity and the luxury of a comparison making the differences stand out. The ruff also returns and this time, being in the hide, we are much closer and are able to see the delicate 'scaly' markings on its back and wings. To complete the waders on view, four black tailed godwits came down to feed. In the short grass around the edge of the scrape, four stock dove were feeding. Once again, something disturbed the peace and the birds took off so we decided it was time we moved on.

Making our way back along a track which had a few patches of shrub either side was where we noticed an increase in the movement and calls of smaller birds. Once again, there were a number of whitethroats, but also goldfinches and one or two unidentified birds that quickly flew from bush to bush and each time concealed themselves. Then two birds flew to the top of a stunted hawthorn and allowed us time to focus our telescopes; they were whinchats. Both were juveniles, only hatched probably a month or two ago making their way to Africa -what an undertaking.

We walked another mile or more back to the car and drove to the nearby 'White Lion' pub for lunch. Had we been birding or birdwatching? Who cares!

A view from the hide, across the scrape with the refinery in the background

Protecting My Nuts!
September 2007

Thirty give years ago, my wife bought a foot high shrub from Notcutt's nursery and planted it in our garden. Five years later, we moved house and dug up what was by now a small tree and transported it in our Vauxhall Viva to our present home. The upheaval did not seem to harm our twisted hazel (Corylus avellana "Contorta") as it is now around fifteen feet high and twelve feet across.

Maybe it is because I have watched the tree slowly grow over the years that I find myself becoming increasingly protective of the hazel nut crop. It is in August that I start to get nervous; the nuts are mainly green with one or two only just starting to turn brown and for the last couple of years this has heralded the visit of a grey squirrel. How do they know? I rarely see one in the garden at any other time of the year(do they remember?). Telltale piles of green husks on the ground near to the tree are usually the first signs of the unwelcome furry visitor.

The squirrel soon became used to my tactics of charging out of the back door waving my hands and would, on occasions, simply retreat to a safer place in the adjacent apple or bay tree and look nonchalantly down at me. Feeling insulted, I armed myself with a 10' garden cane which I kept handy by the back door and when called into action I would rush across the lawn and jab the cane at the retreating squirrel as it disappeared into the trees. Despite my desperate tactics, I would watch the nuts slowly disappear.

It was last year, while I was on 'sentry duty', that I discovered that the squirrel was not the only one plundering my nut crop. I watched in disbelief as a great spotted woodpecker landed on the tree, selected a nut and flew off with it in its beak - only to return about 10 minutes later for another. Was this the same woodpecker that less than a week ago was content with almost daily visits to my peanut feeder but now, almost overnight, it appears its tastes have changed? The peanut feeder is full, the nearby beech tree groaning with mast but both, it seems, do not have the same attraction as my hazelnuts.

This year the squirrel did not turn up but the woodpecker was bolder than ever. She (it is always a female that I see) would herald her intentions by calling from the very top of the beech tree and, although I would only rarely see her on the hazel tree, I came to know when she had struck. It was the tap-tap-tap sound coming from the beech tree that gave it away. Through binoculars I could see her drumming on what must have been hazelnuts, as it was always in exactly the same position and she appeared to be using the flattish surface of a previously pruned branch as a workbench. Some days, the tap-tap-tapping was the first indication of a visit and, as always, she would be busy hammering away in exactly the same spot.

Despite the pillaging by fur and feather, come September I do manage to harvest a handful of nuts for us to eat so I suppose there is some sort of natural balance taking place. I usually give the boughs a shake and any ripe nuts that are left fall to the ground; some are lost amongst the grass and shrubs and even into next door's garden. In winter, I often find empty shells, sometimes in a pile in the corner of the old shed, with a small hole gnawed in the side where I assume the mice have had a meal from the fallen nuts.

The hazel is one of the last trees to lose its leaves in our garden(around mid December) to reveal the next generation of catkins. By the end of February, the small red female flowers (like tiny red tassels on the buds) have opened and, by March, the catkins have doubled in length and have changed to a lighter green/yellow colour. Wind or even birds moving through the bush can cause the pollen to 'puff' from the catkins and, I assume, pollinate the flowers, setting in motion a chain of events that may again result in me waving a stick at a squirrel or woodpecker come August.

My wife tells me to 'get a life'.

The Farmers' Market
November 2007

For a number of years now we have been buying produce from the fortnightly farmers market held at Barleylands Farm, Billericay. Most of the stalls are housed within a large metal 'barn' with a few set up outside around the entrance where there is also a large stationary steam engine chugging away, which I discovered recently, was an old ploughing engine.

The majority of the stall holders are from the East Anglia region and sell their own produce so if you are interested in reducing your 'food miles' or 'carbon footprint' then buying from these types of places will help. Walking around supermarkets I find it unbelievable that we are importing onions from New Zealand, fish from Jamaica, asparagus from Peru and strawberries from the USA. Having said that, most supermarkets now recognise that there is a growing demand for British or locally sourced food and are now providing some 'home' grown products but you still have to look carefully for them.

I think we all need to accept the seasons and not expect tomatoes, asparagus or strawberries all the year round. The next time you are moaning about the number of lorries on our roads just think of all the produce, such as those onions from New Zealand, on their way to your local supermarket after being flown thousands of miles. We can make a difference by buying seasonal local produce.

The market certainly makes you more aware of the changing seasons as some products and stall holders disappear and then return at their allotted

The Farmers' Market

part of the year. You may have to tailor your purchases to go with the time of the year because, for example, the venison stall only sells the meat between October and March and the wild food stall has what are in season i.e. no wild birds in their breeding season. The fishmonger will only briefly be selling samphire and the fish will change with the time of the year. In the autumn a man appears for a couple of months selling nothing but local apples and pears.

Being in direct contact with the producers allows you to ask questions regarding farming practices, fishing methods, animal welfare, how far do the animals have to travel for slaughter or even, how are they slaughtered? They in turn inform you of the problems that they can face such as adverse weather or just lately the twin outbreaks of foot and mouth and bluetongue. Over time we have got to know a number of the stallholders and have on occasions visited their farms; there is still one, with breeding little owls, that we have not yet got round to.

Going back to the wild food stall, I do have to fight with my conscience as to whether I should be buying such food but usually have no problem purchasing rabbit, pigeon, pheasant and partridge (red legged variety only). I will not buy hare or woodcock and often voice my concerns to the stall holder. Then, in the middle, are birds such as mallard and teal where I sway one way and then the other over the decision on whether to buy or not. Is my custom encouraging more shooting or am I merely using up what is killed anyway?

A number of stalls also sell organic produce. I sometimes think that organic produce and organic farming gets some undeserved bad press mainly because some people seem to expect so much more from the produce and miss the point of the production. We buy meat, poultry and eggs from an organic farm and I would say that I cannot always taste the difference between non organic and organic but after a couple of visits to organic farms I know why I choose organic. Organic farms that meet the requirements of the soil association or the organic farm federation (their produce or packaging will display an association logo or a reference number) need to manage a number of issues including looking after the condition of the soil by maintaining levels of organic matter and encouraging soil biological activity. They also control weed, disease and pest control by relying primarily on crop rotations, natural predators, diversity, organic manuring and resistant varieties with the use of minimal chemicals. The management of livestock is also very important, giving full regard to their behavioural needs and welfare with respect to nutrition, housing, health, breeding and rearing. All this must be carried out whilst paying attention to the impact of the farming system on the wider environment and the conservation of wildlife and natural habitats.

The result of these practices seems to show up when you walk around the farms; you are aware that there are fewer animals and chickens, more hedgerows and far more weeds, insects and birds. There is also no doubt that the chickens are truly free range - they were roaming all around the farm. And at least I know that my meat and milk is not injected with antibiotics or hormones and they have not been feeding on fields that have been sprayed with herbicides or pesticides or both.

I have not carried out a detailed price comparison with supermarkets but it is likely that farmers markets are dearer but I think a small reduction in the amount bought quickly adjusts the cost and perhaps we could all do with eating less. I know I could. All said, I am prepared to pay a little extra for organic food; for me it is a another way to assist wildlife and, although not a charity, I see it as being similar to giving a contribution to bodies such as the RSPB or the Woodland Trust.

What a moral maze the comparatively simple undertaking of shopping can be!

Inside the Farmers' Market

Two Tree Island
16th November 2007

After scraping the ice from the wind screen we set off in the morning rush hour traffic of the busy A13 road. The sun was shining as we turned into the road by Leigh-on-Sea railway station, drove over the bridge across Leigh Creek and parked in the relative tranquillity of the first car park on Two Tree Island. Although bright and with little or no wind as we started walking we could feel it was definitely woolly hat and gloves weather.

As we made our way towards the western end of the island a number of small birds were flitting around the bushes or flying overhead, mainly chaffinches and greenfinches but amongst them, one or two reed buntings and meadow pipits. A group of ten to twelve birds were particularly active, flying around in circles or landing in bushes too distant for us to recognise. However with patience and the disturbance by dog walkers the group eventually landed in bushes fairly close by and through our telescopes we could see that they were corn buntings. Considering it is a bird of browns and creamy whites it is rather striking when seen in warm sunlight with the streaky patterns on the wings and breast.

We arrived at the hide overlooking the lagoon at the western end of the island and after opening up a couple of viewing hatches we sat down and scanned the scene with our binoculars. There were plenty of teal and a few widgeon around the edges of the islands, most with their heads tucked in enjoying a snooze in the sunshine. The green speculum of the teal, especially on the female it seems, would sometimes glint vividly when caught in the sunshine. Scanning the extremities of the lagoon we briefly saw a water rail but it moved out of sight beneath the overhanging vegetation on one of the small islands. However, after a short while it reappeared and we were able to watch this rather secretive bird preening before it once again slipped away from view.

To the far right of the lagoon we saw a single snipe probing deep in the mud with its long straight bill looking for food (on that cold morning it seemed a most unappetising way to have to find your food).

It was time to move on and we decided to head back east walking along a track on the southern edge looking out over the saltmarsh and mud of Hadleigh Ray towards Canvey Island. It was low tide and with the sun in our eyes, reflecting off the mud, it was difficult to recognise any waders apart from the distinctive curlew. We soon came to a second hide and despite the sun decided to spend some time scanning the mudflats. I am glad we made the effort because we found a flock of two hundred or more knot along with a few redshank and grey plover. Having a number of wader species together certainly helps with identification, giving you comparisons of size, body shape and behaviour -especially useful when they are all wearing their winter outfits.

We had just left the hide when, not that far from us just above the height of the vegetation, a kestrel and a much larger raptor seemed to almost collide with both birds twisting violently upwards and away in different directions. The larger bird had brown and white plumage and we both initially thought a short eared owl but the distinctive white rump confirmed it was a female hen harrier. We tried to get another sighting but it had disappeared as quickly as it arrived.

The Lagoon on Two Tree Island

On the walk back to the car-park for a hot coffee we saw a number of obliging stonechats (male and female). Suitably warmed, we now continued to the east of the island. Here I got my first sighting of a 'winter thrush', a redwing. Walking further along the path, something stopped us in our tracks: it was the sight of three furry animals in a tree eating crab apples. They were brown rats and they did not seem to be bothered by us watching their antics from fairly close by. We looked on fascinated as they rather clumsily moved around the branches reaching out or hanging down to take a large bite out of an apple which they would then eat by holding the piece in their paws while sitting on their haunches just like a squirrel nibbling a nut. We took a number of photographs of these creatures who are normally seen as nocturnal scavengers around human habitation and waste but here in the sunshine they looked an entirely different animal.

Moving on, we came across another hide looking out over a small pool (which I later found out was an old sewage works); here were a number of mallard, shoveler, teal and a pair of dabchicks. Then, to our surprise, another water rail appeared, this time much closer and we were able to clearly see the black and white barring on the flanks the blue-grey underparts, the warm streaky brown back and long red bill and eye. Funny, I haven't seen a water rail in years and then along come two in one day!

We reach the eastern most point of the path and look out at the Thames estuary, and then the pubs in Leigh and decide its time for lunch. In 'The Old Smack' in Leigh old town we sat at a table looking out over the river and watched numerous brent geese drifting in on the tide. Much closer, little egrets and turnstones were feeding on the edge of the advancing water. What a finish to an interesting day!

A brown rat eating an apple

Bird Behaviour in Brighton
February 2008

In February, my wife and I decided on a short break in Brighton and, despite the city environs, we still came across two instances of interesting bird behaviour.

The first was of a well documented and often filmed occurrence in other parts of the country, that we witnessed whilst strolling along the seafront. It was getting near to dusk when I started to notice flocks of fifty to a hundred starlings flying over the sea just off the beach towards Brighton's pier. As we watched, the flocks seemed to be getting bigger with some up to a thousand in my estimation. We could see that the flocks were combining and forming larger flocks that were swirling around the length of the pier. Eager to get a better look, we quickened our pace towards the pier, as we did more flocks passed us to join the throng. When we reached the pier and looked westward, silhouetted against the setting sun and the pastel colours of the evening sky some stragglers were still winging their way towards us. Along the pier, the main flock, which must have numbered close to five thousand, was indulging in aerial acrobatics as it rose up and then swept under the pier, fragmenting as individuals broke away to claim their roosting spot; the remainder regrouped into an ever changing mass ready for another fly past. Each time the main body of birds swept below the pier, fewer would reappear as they slowly found somewhere to roost. As we walked along the pier, you could hear the twittering and squeaking of the birds below the wooden boards and sometimes, if you peered through gaps, you could see them on the iron framework. It did amaze me that that the birds were not put off by the multitude of lights or the number of people strolling along the pier and found a roosting site over the cold grey English channel cosy enough to want to spend the night. But it must have suited them because eventually even the stragglers had found a place and no more birds could be seen on the wing. Maybe the weather conditions need to be just right as the next evening, armed this time with a camera, we positioned ourselves on the pier awaiting the display and, of course, they turned up in far, far, fewer numbers.

These gatherings of starlings known as a 'murmuration' have a number of benefits for the birds. The grouping together offers protection from predators such as peregrine falcons or sparrowhawks who find it disorientating to pick a victim from the swirling thousands. Huddling together also helps to keep them warm through the cold winter nights and maybe exchange information on the best feeding locations.

The second event was in the gardens around the Brighton pavilion. We came across two immaculate adult herring gulls on the lawn in the shadow of the pavilion. I am not sure what it was that made us take notice but we could see that they were moving in an odd way. As we walked closer we could make out that both birds, either individually or in unison, were rhythmically drumming the ground with their pink feet for periods of around ten seconds. Often after a burst of drumming on the spot, the birds would thrust their beaks into the grass just in front of their feet and they certainly appeared to be feeding on something. I am sure that on some occasions they pulled up worms. The birds remained in the same area not moving more that two foot either way and staying approximately two foot apart... On occasions they faced us side by side and started the rapid tap dancing which was comical looking and prompted my wife to say it looked like the theatre show, 'Riverdance'. Our observations were unfortunately halted after approximately fifteen minutes by what sounded like someone dropping a large sheet of metal that made the gulls take to the wing. What were they doing? My wife wondered if they were imitating the sound of falling rain that maybe encouraged worms to the surface. It sounded a good theory to me! Further investigations proved that my wife's theory that they were attracting worms was indeed correct and that herring gulls are not the only species of bird to adopt this technique.

Brighton Pier

A Mixed Bag on Fobbing Marsh
August 2008

Despite the grey skies and the forecast of rain, Ken, Mick and I decided to go ahead with a walk over the Fobbing marshes. Whether it was due to having had very little use for them on a couple of previous windswept days on the marsh, or maybe we are just becoming lazier, but today we decided to leave our telescopes at home. Mick did not even bring his binoculars, so I was beginning to think that today would be the day when a rare bird turns up and we would not get a good look at it.

Not far from the footpath in a small fenced off field where the grass was longer, Ken remarked that this looked like an ideal place to find wasp spiders as he had seen one recently at Rainham marshes in similar habitat. I had only just replied that they had also been reported at Benfleet when, unbelievably, I saw my first wasp spider on its web not three foot away. And what a sight it was! A large, striking yellow and black spider, sitting in the middle of its web with two pairs of long, menacing banded front legs. Intriguingly, each web had a thicker strand in the shape of a 'squiggle' which we have since been unable to find out its purpose.

Within five minutes we had found a total of five webs with spiders in a small area and because we might trample or damage further webs we moved on, keeping to the areas of shorter grass. I am sure that there were more webs in the area. It would appear that judging by the various reports of sightings in South Essex, 2008 has been a good year for these aptly named spiders.

We hadn't walked far when we came across an old wooden pallet leaning up against a bramble

Wasp spider

bush. Then someone noticed a cricket slowly making its way up the pallet. We just managed to get a photograph before our views were obscured by bramble. It was a great green bush cricket and must have been two and a half inches long- truly a giant among crickets.

Despite the cloudy and windy weather, there were a good number of butterflies on the wing in the more sheltered spots. common blues, meadow browns and gatekeepers were the most numerous with single marbled white and wall brown.

When we arrived at the 'scrape', around seven house martins flew overhead and, on the mud, four green sandpipers and seven black tailed godwits were feeding but quickly took to the wing on our approach. As we continued, a brown hare startled from the long grass nearby and bolted away, disappearing from sight as it descended into a dry ditch.

Walking back along the main track from the scrape we found an old sheet of rusting corrugated iron lying by some bramble and while the others got their cameras ready I got hold of the sheet. During the walk we had lifted three or four pieces of various flat material and had only found a total of three slowworms. When they were ready I lifted the sheet and underneath was an adder. It must have been content as it did not move while we took photos and then carefully replaced the metal sheet.

As we continued on back, we could see a police helicopter circling over the Manorway and a number of blue flashing lights at the road. When we arrived at the roundabout, a security man appeared and told us that environmental protesters were expected at the refinery. I think he initially thought we might be part of the protest.

A great green bush-cricket

We found out later that the protesters did, in fact, target Kingsnorth Power Station in Kent. They were protesting against a plan to replace the existing coal fired station with a new coal fired one, saying this and other proposals at coal fired sites will prevent the UK from meeting carbon reduction targets.

As we drove away only one or two police cars were evident and no flashing lights could been seen. Further along the road, we stopped for bacon sandwiches and reflected on the fact that we had not needed our telescopes , there were no rare birds today.

I sometimes think that birdwatchers often miss others forms wildlife because we are invariably looking to the distance or upwards rather than what is close at hand. So maybe the lack of telescopes made us concentrate more on other forms of wildlife.

An adder on Fobbing Marsh

A Magic Moment
October 2008

We had just come home from shopping and, as I looked out through the kitchen door to the garden, I saw around five house sparrows bathing in the birdbath with two or three on the side patiently awaiting their turn. Streams of droplets were spraying in all directions as they dipped their bodies, fluffed up their feathers and joyously flapped and shook their wings. The low afternoon sunlight behind the bathers caught the flying beads of water so that they sparkled, illuminating this social scene of whirling wings and splashing water in the collective delight of cleansing their feathers.

In Search of Redpolls
December 2009

It was minus two degrees centigrade as we set off in the dark for Thorndon Park. When we arrived in the gloom the warden was trying to open the frozen lock on the car park gate so our headlights assisted him in completing the task. We parked the car and I walked to the pay machine (yes, you pay to park there) but is was too dark to see or read the buttons so decided it would also be too dark to see birds and retreated back to the car. As the pale wash of light on the horizon spread and grew brighter I managed to find the slot for my £2 and punch the frozen button and the machine whirled and delivered a ticket.

We had been here, trying to find the redpolls, ten days previously on a Saturday morning but we did not arrive until 10 am, by then the park was very busy with dog walkers, joggers and cyclists and reports had said it was best to be here early. Needless to say we did not see any redpolls.

Now, all was silent in the wood and the only sound we could hear was the faint crackling of the frosty ground beneath our feet and not a sign of a dog walker. The grass was white with the heavy frost and the sky to the east was gaining some faint pink and yellow to go with the cold blue light as we walked along looking for signs of small birds feeding in the birch trees. Up to now we had only heard the occasional call from a blackbird or a robin so it almost made me jump when quite a 'large' bird suddenly broke noisily from a clump of dead brown bracken right by my feet. As this predominantly brown bird with darker markings on its back flew away low on broad wings and zig zagged through the trees we could see it was a woodcock, the first I have seen for a number of years.

After walking on for another fifteen minutes or so we spotted some small birds in the trees but they turned out to be a flock of mainly long tailed tits but it did contain at least one coal tit. Encouraged, we strolled on and after around fifteen minutes spotted two or three birds in a birch tree and with telescopes we could see the red patch on the crown, the small black bib and confirmed they were indeed redpolls After watching them for a while there turned out to be in fact six birds but what type? Now my lesson on identification started, were they lesser, mealy, arctic, or plain old common redpoll? What with the alternative names I was not even sure what to call them. My friend was trying to point out how two of the birds were much paler and the streaking along their flanks was going farther back, therefore they were likely to be mealy redpolls, or should I call them common redpolls? The other birds seemed slightly smaller and darker and were deemed to be lesser redpolls. The debates over these birds will I am sure rumble on, looking for such small differences in characteristics or plumage is not easy, especially on such an active bird often viewed in the very tops of trees. As for me I was happy that I had seen a redpoll!

Our quest however was not over, recent reports had mentioned a flock of around two hundred redpolls had been seen and we thought that would indeed be a sight to behold and maybe an opportunity to compare any differences in rarer individuals. That said we had been out in the freezing cold for around two hours and we were now close to the car park once again and decided on a warming coffee break. Revitalised, we headed back into the woods in search of the 'flock and soon met another birdwatcher, telescope over shoulder, who told us that he had recently seen a flock of around fifty redpolls but before he had had a good look they were disturbed and took flight, joining a bigger flock that was moving overhead. Having received directions we once again set off amongst the birches seeking the big flock. However our next find came not from continuously craning our necks skywards but from looking at the floor of the wood in order not to trip over some fallen birch, it was a perfect fly agaric. This beautiful but poisonous classic bright red mushroom with white 'warts' stood out against the carpet of copper coloured leaves and lo and behold my book says that it is found beneath birch trees. Perfect!

A short while later we met the same birdwatcher and again he had seen the flock of more than fifty redpolls but they had flown, however he still gave us directions. When we arrived at the spot there was indeed no sign of redpolls so we decided to make our way back to the car park via the tarmac track which had plenty of birch trees on either side. As we walked along the track around twenty small birds flew over and settled in the top of a birch tree set back from the track, partly obscured by other trees. The trees were on private land so we set up our telescopes by the pathway and could see they were redpolls and as we looked more joined them but at that moment a car came along and the flock lifted off which at least gave us a chance to estimate that the flock was around sixty birds, not the two hundred we were hoping for. They settled in trecs on our side of the track for around thirty seconds before they were off again, returning to almost the same area we first saw them, but once again just as they seemed to be settling down another car came along and the birds once again took flight this time disappearing out of sight.

By now it was nearly 10 am and still only just above freezing so we decided to call it a day and get the car heater on as soon as possible.

Fly Agaric mushroom

Stalking a Night Heron
January 2009

A friend of mine, who subscribes to an organisation that sends out news of sightings of rare birds and their locations to his pager, had proposed that we go to see a night heron that had been reported as being present in a small reed bed on a canal, for the past couple of weeks.

Given the title, I suppose it was appropriate for us to leave while it was still dark. We joined the continuous line of car rear lights on the main A13 road and crossed the QE11 bridge heading down to darkest Kent. This was my first real 'twitch' outside of Essex.

By the time we arrived at the car park beside the Royal Military Canal in West Hythe, it was light and, after the warmth of the car, it felt very cold. According to the directions we had, it was about a half a mile walk along the canal bank to the area that the bird was last seen. As we walked along the canal path, we caught a glimpse of two small birds with white rumps as they flew from bushes on our side of the canal to trees on the other bank. Then we could see they were bullfinches.

Before long we reached the spot where the heron was last seen. We cannot claim any prizes for finding the bird for, as we arrived, a birdwatcher was just leaving and he pointed out the bird sulking in the small reed-bed on the other side of the canal. We quickly set up our telescopes and we were soon looking at my first night heron.

What was this bird doing here, hunched in the sparse, dry brown remnants of last year's reeds, with its pale yellow toes in the cold water? It was around four degrees centigrade with the wind blowing across the flat bleak Romney Marsh, the water on our side of the canal frozen in places up to a distance of three feet from the bank, a far different scene from the heron's normal wintering grounds in Africa.

The night heron is smaller than our own grey heron with a short thick neck, large head and stout bill. This being an adult bird, it is rather striking with its black crown and back, grey wings and white underparts. We were close enough to see its rather large bead-like black eyes with an amber outer ring.

As we watched the motionless bird seemingly concentrating its stare at the water immediately in front of it, we were suddenly jolted out of our gaze by the flash of its bill as it stabbed at a fish. And what a fish it was. It seemed about half the size of the bird as it was initially lifted clear of the water before dropping back and our first thoughts were that it was a large flounder. The heron made two or three more stabs at the fish as it thrashed around in the reeds and weed before it escaped to deeper water. I think the bird was surprised at the size of its prey and I am sure that it would never have been able to swallow such a large fish even if it had managed to keep it. With that over, the heron resumed its hunched vigil.

After that burst of excitement, we decided to walk further along the bank of the canal in search of kingfishers. The canal was built at the time of the Napoleonic Wars and from where we stood it was dead straight for around three hundred yards yards before a 'dog-leg' in the path. A passing local informed us that the canal was constructed with a series of straight runs of this distance before a 'kink' as this was the range of a musket when fired, we wondered was this fact or fiction? Any way we walked the length of travel of a musket ball but did not see any kingfishers.

On retracing our steps we met another birdwatcher and duly passed on the position of the heron.

As we drove home I could not help but think of the night heron so far from its normal range, will it make it back home? Then a discussion started on what type of fish it was that it so nearly caught and as we concluded that the water was fresh and not brackish or salt then the fish was unlikely to be a flounder but more likely a bream. Whatever fish it was, it appears to have the skill and the prey available, so hopefully it will at least not go hungry. After all, the canal also appeals to little egret and grey heron which we had also seen today.

A night heron in Kent

Winter Wonders from a Window
February 2009

I know winter has many negatives but one positive for a birdwatcher is that the cold weather often brings rather more unusual birds to the garden. So far, 2009 has been exceptional for not only low temperatures but also the heaviest snow falls for 18 years and, this time, Essex has not escaped lightly as is often the case.

The New Year started well with temperatures below zero at night and on New Year's day a woodcock flew into the garden and, unbelievably, landed on the patio outside the back door, strolling past not six feet away from me. It was so close that I could see the beautifully delicate brown and black markings of its plumage, its rather strange shaped head and long bill. The best view I have ever had!

The first week in January saw overnight temperatures dropping and, by the end of the week, it was down to -5°C; in fact, our doorstep milk was frozen- something I had not seen in years. The cold had certainly increased the number of birds in the garden with more than the usual numbers of woodpigeons, chaffinches, greenfinches and up to eight blackbirds on the lawn, often squabbling and chasing one another. On the two days when there was a light covering of snow, visits from the song thrush and great spotted woodpecker increased. This month also saw more than normal sightings of long tailed tits passing through in groups, with perhaps the best sight being when three of the birds managed to hang on a fat ball at once, with 2 or 3 others awaiting their turn on adjacent branches. Towards the end of the month, temperatures did rise somewhat and we even had rain; in fact, on the day I took part in the RSPB great garden birdwatch the wind and rain meant I recorded very few birds in my allotted hour despite putting out lots of goodies for them to eat.

The milder weather did not last long and on the 2nd of February we awoke to two to three inches of snow triggering a veritable bonanza for my garden bird year list. The first unusual bird to appear was a goldcrest and it was just outside the patio window, systematically searching for food amongst the shrubs, its golden flash in the middle of the crown could be clearly seen. I went outside to clear the snow off the bird-table and to sweep away the snow from an area in the middle of the lawn and below two feeders hanging from shrubs in the border. After throwing handfuls of wildbird seed and crushed peanuts on the cleared areas and onto the bird-table, I retreated to the warmth of indoors and waited with my binoculars at hand. It wasn't long before the chaffinches came for the seed on the ground and they were quickly joined by house sparrows that were now torn between the feeders and what was on offer on the ground. Next, the blackbirds appeared, bounding down the garden through the snow to join in the feast and occasionally lunging at one another. The presence of other birds seemed to give the dunnocks confidence because two of them appeared from nowhere and worked their way along the edge of the lawn paying particular attention to the cleared areas below the feeders. A pied wagtail joined in and spent some time searching for suitable food before they appeared to be sent packing by the boisterous blackbirds. A little later, another member of the wagtail family flew down to the cleared area, I couldn't believe my eyes: it was a grey wagtail -the first I had seen in the garden. The bird had greyish upperparts, whitish on the breast and a very long, 'bouncing' tail but what caught my eye was the lemon yellow on the vent area, I am not sure if it was the snow but the yellow seemed dazzling it was so bright. It only stayed a few minutes and it was gone. phew!

Just before midday, the snow started to fall again and then, just to enhance the scene, two large thrushes landed in the bare branches of a tall shrub not ten foot' from the patio window. With my binoculars I had some fantastic close-up views of two fieldfares and was able to see their beautifully streaked orange/ochre throats and the brown scalloped streaking on their flanks. As they sat there with their feathers fluffed up against the cold, they appeared to have been attracted by some red berries on a Guelder Rose (Viburnum opulus) growing in our neighbours' garden, but hanging over our garden but, before they made a move, a song thrush arrived and started to eat the berries. It was a sight I never imagined that I would see in my back garden, two fieldfares and a song thrush close together, framed with a few red berries and the falling snow. Further down the garden, another thrush caught my eye and (as I almost expected) it was a redwing, I could see clearly the rust-red on its side and its facial pattern.

I am not sure if it was the white glare of the snow and the matt grey of the sky but all the birds seemed brighter than usual. The starlings looked stunning with their gold spangled, green-blue plumage, the collared dove took on a pinky hue and as for the male chaffinch, great tits and the wood pigeons - they all looked immaculate.

Then on the 4th February with the snow still on the ground, I could see that down the garden was a song thrush with something in its bill and when I looked through my binoculars I could confirm that it was a snail. The thrush then proceeded to dash the snail on its 'anvil' which, in this case, was the concrete path in front of the greenhouse. After several hefty blows, the flesh of the snail was exposed and eaten in hurried gulps before a nearby blackbird came to investigate. Although on the odd occasions I have found broken snail shells in the garden this was the first time I had ever witnessed the act.

By the 6th of February the snow in the garden was almost gone and, unfortunately, so were most of the birds but I am still left with the house sparrows, the squabbling blackbirds, the dainty chaffinches and, of course, the collared doves.

One bird that I did expect to see in the snow but did not, was the robin; after all, it's always there in the snowy scenes on Christmas cards!

Our garden in the snow

Old Hall Marshes
March 2009

I know I shouldn't do it but whenever I go birdwatching I nearly always think that I would like to see this or that particular species and then, at the end of the day, when I fail to do so there can be a touch of sadness. Not just because I have failed to see the chosen bird but because it usually means I have picked a bird that is shrinking in numbers and drawing a blank just seems to highlight its predicament. And so it was that when we set out for Old Hall Marshes a friend and I had both said that we hoped to see a grey partridge, a bird that I haven't seen for a good few years. Now perhaps Old Hall Marshes is not the best place to see them but there had been recent sightings and so the expectation was set.

The grey partridge (Perdix perdix) is a bird of open farmland. Smaller than a pheasant, plump with a small head, short legs and a short tail. Well camouflaged, with brown and grey streaked plumage, chestnut bars on its flanks and a grey breast. The face is orangey/brown and it has a dark brown horseshoe shaped mark on its belly. The female is slightly smaller with a less obvious horseshoe mark. The bird is resident, rarely moving more than a few kilometres from where it hatched. It prefers open areas of low grass with dense cover for nesting and dry areas for dust bathing and are most numerous where there is both pasture and cereal fields with thick hedges. It benefits from uncultivated areas, wide (unsprayed) field margins and stubble fields in winter. According to the RSPB, during the last twenty five years the British population has fallen by a massive 84% and the species is also declining in other parts of Europe.

The destruction of hedgerows and the changes in farming practices including the use of chemicals are thought to be the main reasons for the decline. It is now estimated that there are now around seventy five thousand pairs in Britain.

As we left the car park (you need to apply for a pass to visit and use the car park at this RSPB reserve), we hoped for a glimpse of just one of those estimated one hundred and fifty thousand individuals. For the moment though, all thoughts of the partridge were put aside as we walked further into the reserve and the areas of open water, reeds and grazing marsh stretched out before us and we could hear the sound of wigeon 'whistling' and the incessant murmur from thousands of brent geese in the distance. It was a bright sunny day with a brisk wind cold enough to sting the ears and make your eyes water when using the 'scope but at least the sunlight brought out the best in the landscape and the wildlife. On the water, or resting on the margins, with their heads tucked in were large numbers of ducks. They included colourful shelducks with their bright red bills, teal (the vibrantly marked males contrasting with the camouflage of the females) and, perhaps the smartest of all, the male pintail with its chocolate brown head and upper neck with a narrow white stripe running up from the breast through the brown. Tufted ducks and pochard were there in smaller numbers, along with two or three great crested grebes and little grebes. On the grasslands, sheep were not the only creatures grazing, flocks of wigeon were constantly moving over the ground, occasionally disappearing in patches of longer grass or behind the numerous hummocks containing the nests of the yellow meadow ants.

A 'Birder' at Old Hall Marshes

For sheer numbers of grazers though you could not beat the brent geese; there must have been over two thousand of these winter visitors and when occasionally they were either disturbed or perhaps needed to find a fresh patch of vegetation to nibble, the flock lifted in a noisy clamour of calls and wingbeats. Watching them feeding, you notice the constant movement of the flock as they jostle for the best patches of grass while constantly calling. They were not the only geese on the reserve.We also saw small groups of greylag geese and canada geese both keeping to themselves and well away from the hordes of the smaller brents. Sharing the space with the brent geese, and not seeming to mind the noise or the crowds, were a number of lapwing and around a dozen ruff.

Away from the madding crowd, just above a distant patch of reeds we saw the slow 'clipped' wing beats of a marsh harrier as it hunted. Then a little later we saw another two marsh harriers higher in the sky performing what might be described as an aerial display with much chasing, twisting and turning. One was certainly a female; darker with a straw coloured crown but the other bird did not seem as pale as would be expected for a male? Perhaps it was an argument rather than courtship?

The path took us up onto the seawall giving us good views along the Salcott Channel. The tide was out so there were large areas of mud with only a narrow stretch of water remaining. Along the water's edge were a variety of waders including the tiny busy dunlins, more ruffs, redshanks, bar tailed godwits, black tailed godwits, one or two oystercatchers, grey plover, greenshank and on the water one duck, a female goldeneye. We continued walking along the seawall and scanned the fields beyond the creek, still looking for partridges, but instead we did see three brown hares and a number of new born lambs.

We arrived back at the car park without seeing a grey partridge but pleased with the sights and sounds of our four hour stroll. There was nothing else left but to indulge in another favourite pastime of mine - sampling the local beer; so we stopped off at the Queen's Head in Tolleshunt D'Arcy for a pint of Adnams' 'Broadside'. After all, we do need to support our country pubs especially in these times of recession:two pubs have already closed in the village. While supping I resolved to keep trying to find a grey partridge in Essex and reflected on the contrasting success of the deliberately introduced red-legged partridge (RSPB estimate 1.5 million individuals in Britain). Admittedly that figure includes those that are raised and released in time for shooting. So why not rear grey partridges? Some are bound to survive and maybe numbers could slowly recover in Essex?

The lagoon at Old Hall Marshes

Seeking a Grey Partridge
April 2009

This year a friend and I have become somewhat preoccupied with seeing a grey partridge in Essex. Why a grey partridge and why specifically in Essex? With me I think it was simple nostalgia. I am sure I remember seeing them locally in East Tilbury and Stanford Le Hope and it would be uplifting to know that they still survived in our area, despite the ever encroaching tide of concrete driven by an expanding population. But what I think really set us looking was when a friend of mine (who I am sure will not mind if I describe him as a 'twitcher') remarked that it was a bird missing from his extensive Essex list.

Judging by the lack of reported sightings around the county on various 'birder' forums and websites on the internet, we were obviously not the only ones struggling to find this now elusive bird of open arable farmland. Conversations with other birdwatchers in the field confirmed the RSPB's view that this bird has suffered a drastic decline and the general consensus was that this is now a difficult bird to locate.

As recounted in the article preceding this, of the few reported sightings most were around the north of the county and in one place in particular, Old Hall Marshes, they seemed to be regular but sporadic. We did visit the site but failed to see a partridge but after talking to another pair of birdwatchers who said they had been to Old Hall around twenty times and had never seen one, we realised our attempt was indeed a weak effort. So, despite a number of outings to various birdwatching sites where we have endeavoured to look in any adjacent fields, the bird had remained elusive.

However, my friend is part of an internet group of Essex birdwatchers and he asked the group for information on any sites where grey partridge had recently been seen. Only four sites were suggested and two of those were for Old Hall Marshes but, interestingly, the others were much closer to home; one in Grays and one in Orsett. Armed with this new information, we decided to try our luck.

I awoke at around 6.30 and, looking out the window, saw that it was very misty with visibility down to a few hundred yards. Not a good start for going birdwatching but the forecast was for a fine sunny day so when my friend picked me up at 09.00 we both agreed that it would clear sooner or later. Following the directions given, we stopped in a car park next to a block of flats in Grays and walked a well worn path through a hedge onto the approach road to the Thurrock Rugby Club. On the other side of the road there was a cereal field where partridges had been seen; it stretched out before us, the end of which we could not see because of the mist. The mist rolled back and forth with the tussle between the breeze and the obscured sun slowly warming the air. Scanning the field, our imaginations often took over. "Was that a head, what's that darker patch?" It was only a pigeon! But no partridge. It dawned on us that most of the cereal in this field was of a height that would hide a partridge completely and the odds on a fox, which we could see at the edge of the field, flushing a partridge in our direction were far too long so we moved on.

Walking back to the public road we crossed over and stepped through a large gap in the hedge and followed a well worn path between two other expansive cereal fields, stopping now and again to survey the scene with our binoculars and quite often catching sight of something grey and moving. Unfortunately, these turned out to be mostly rabbits of various sizes, nibbling their way around the edges or wood pigeons startled by our presence. As we walked, occasionally having to avoid the dog's mess, skylarks were calling overhead and the sun started to break through. At the other side of the fields we entered an area of rough grass and bushes which did not look suitable for partridges and so, after a quick 'scan' for the elusive bird, we backtracked to the road.

We decided to carry on down the narrow single track 'no through road' towards the A13, looking through or peering over the hedges either side into the adjacent fields. The green of the hedgerows were violated at regular intervals by fly-tipped rubbish, a lay-by was rendered unusable by unwanted items of modern day society, including a brightly coloured child's gun, garden waste and black plastic sacks of unimaginable contents. We marveled at the strength required to dump an armchair over the hedge and into the field at this lonely spot. As we walked we discussed the type of people responsible for this mess and what must go through their minds to justify their actions. By now, the mist had lifted completely and the sun was out - but still no partridge.

Moving on, we could now hear the low incessant rumble of traffic on the old A13 and the road to Tilbury docks and somewhere a dog was continually barking. We came to another gap in the hedge and as I stepped into the entrance to the field I could see what I was sure was a partridge. I called to my friend and put my binoculars to my eyes and it was! To our delight we could both clearly see the orange face, grey neck and front, with chestnut barring on the flanks but that was not all - there was a second grey partridge. What helped was that the cereal in this field was only 3-4 inches high, affording us good views. Now and again they would crouch a little but they were not completely hidden. We could not determine whether they where male or female as the height of the cereal mostly obscured the horseshoe mark on the lower breast which is more pronounced in the male. Also the difference in size could not be ascertained because of the distance between the two birds (the male is larger). Then, a red legged partridge came into view with its distinctive white face enabling us to compare the two species.

We could not believe our luck as we watched the birds quietly searching for food with the occasional look in our direction to make sure we were not coming any nearer. Then, while we must have been watching the nearer bird, the other one disappeared. We are sure it did not fly and thought that maybe it had found a depression in the ground or had taken refuge in the longer coarse grass that was growing beneath the foot of the towering pylon carrying the buzzing cables high across the field. Nevertheless, we were very happy that we had completed our quest and not wanting to disturb them anymore we walked back up the road.

Encouraged by our success, we decided to try the second site in Orsett where partridges had been reported. We stopped at a couple of locations along Conways Lane and surveyed the adjacent fields and, as before, there were no signs of partridge but plenty of rabbits. Then, in the last field before the lane meets the A128, my friend saw a bird sitting on a fence post; to our surprise, it was a buzzard. We had been watching the bird for a few minutes when it flew from the fence, drifted across the field and landed in the shadows of the hedgerow alongside the A128. Shortly, it re-emerged and flew low back across the field with prey in its talons and we were almost sure it was a young rabbit. Unfortunately the bird flew on and out of sight into a clump of trees. Who would have thought that such a wildlife drama would have been acted out to a background of traffic noise, just yards from a busy road? At this point we decided that we had probably seen all the partridges we were likely to for one day and so joined the traffic and headed home.

While there is no doubt that the grey partridge is a Red List Species, I wonder if these birds are perhaps under-reported as to find them you have to spend time looking in arable fields which is not the favourite location for most observers. I am sure that the majority of birdwatchers spend far more time looking in woods, along hedgerows, around reservoirs and along coastlines all of which are normally rather more productive species-wise than the rather sterile open agricultural landscape. Also, the day highlighted the value of people watching their local patch even if those areas are not well known or are less picturesque. After all, if it wasn't for the information we received from that birdwatcher it is most unlikely that we would have chosen that location to go birdwatching and therefore we would still be searching for the Essex grey partridge.

Fennel Feast
August 2009

Last year, quite unremarkably, we grew a few fennel plants (Foeniculum vulgare) from seed in our front garden. This year, as if from nowhere, we have watched one plant, not far from our front door, grow and grow until it reached around ten foot in height with, at the base, eight stems of around 1" diameter and the numerous flower heads spreading out to form an 'umbrella' almost six foot across. Fennel is a very architectural plant with its angular branched stems, plate-like umbelliferous flower heads and the fine wispy leaves below. The tiny, discreet yellow flowers would seem to be so small that it would not be worth the effort to collect or feed from them; whatever it is it certainly attracts numerous insects but, strangely, no bees or butterflies!

The predominant insects were wasps. At times, there must have been around a hundred of them constantly on the move from flower to flower with barely a pause and then flitting to the next flower head. Occasionally, wasp would come into contact with wasp, resulting in a brief aerial skirmish before they would untangle themselves and resume the feast on the flower heads. Certain individual wasps though looked to have a different agenda and seemed to spend more time trying to scare or knock other insects (including other wasps) off the flowers. It turned out to be more sinister than that! Further observations revealed that certain wasps were not interested in what the flowers had to offer and had more carnivorous intentions. These individuals tended to fly below the flower heads then sweep upwards and pounce on some unsuspecting insect feeding on the flowers. In most cases, the intended victim would escape but occasionally the wasp would firmly grasp its prey and fly under the flower heads and, hanging upside down, would start to devour its meal. It was always a fly that was caught and the wasp would bend its abdomen as if stinging its prey. Whether it was my presence or not , the wasp would always fly off with its prey and not stay to finish its meal on the fennel.

Despite the dangers, hoverflies were always well represented. The hoverflies came in various sizes and forms, some even 'dressed' as wasps and trying to differentiate between them while they are constantly on the move, feeding on flowers swaying in the wind or being disturbed by dive–bombing wasps proved beyond my skill and patience. Adding to the insectivorous mix were a number of flies; mainly greenbottles but also some smaller and darker, all painstakingly moving from one small flower to the next. Occasionally there would be one or two ichneumon (I just love that word!) flies - sorry but I do not know which ones; they never stay long enough for me to identify.

Aside from the frenetic activity of the wasps and flies, ladybirds were also there in good numbers. I counted around fifty of various size and spottiness (pretty sad to count them, I know). I could not see what they were feeding on but they seemed more content around the stalks of the flowers or the buds of ex-flowers rather than the flowers themselves.

Later, as the flowers began to fade, I noticed that another insect had taken up residence - a spider, and his larder seemed full; while feasting on one meal, two are wrapped in silken web for later.

The whole scene was one of constant movement, full of energy and variety, all taking place right outside my front door and so far I am happy to report no stings! Although gazing intently at fennel in your front garden can of course leave you open to comments such as "it's no good just looking at it" from passing neighbours. Others will probably think you are just a bit odd and decide to keep their thoughts to themselves.

Of course it is not only the insects that can enjoy the plant. We are still using the dry fennel seeds from last year both as an extra flavouring to toppings of shop bought pizzas or an additional seed in the bread maker. The TV chef Hugh Fearnley-Whittingstall recently recommended throwing the stalks and leaves on to the BBQ coals to allow the aniseed flavour to permeate the food. We have certainly stuffed fish with fennel leaves and lemon before wrapping in a foil parcel and cooking either in the oven or on the barbie. In one cookbook I read that the pollen is also used in cooking and gives a more intense flavour to food. Must be a pain to collect and I would guess the insects might have something to say about that.

When I try to write up these observations it makes me realise how little I know but that does not detract from my enjoyment of watching nature. Sometimes it makes me seek further information or just say to myself "I wonder". Sometimes I surmise what may be happening but would love somebody to confirm or give alternative explanations. At least on occasions it fires me enough to write about it and maybe collectively the gaps in my knowledge can be filled by other members of BNHS.

1. Is it pollen they are collecting or eating?

2. Are some wasps carnivorous?

3. Are the wasps taking their prey somewhere else and if so - why?

Just for a Moment
September 2009

In September, my wife and I were walking along an almost deserted beach in Southern Brittany watching a few locals probing around the rocks and the wet sand with an array of implements looking for various forms of shellfish exposed by the retreating tide.

As usual, I had my binoculars slung around my neck and so I decided to take a closer look at the swallows skimming low around the waters edge. As I followed a particular bird with my binoculars I saw in the background a little egret, its white plumage standing out against the nearby dark rocks. Focusing on the egret, I noticed another bird just to the left; it was larger than the egret and, once I saw its bill, I immediately recognised it and I couldn't believe my eyes! It was an ibis and not just one but three, all slowly searching amongst the rocks and pools for food.

Although I have never seen one in the 'field' before, the distinctive large dark down-curved bill was diagnostic- it had to be an ibis. Now I was really excited, I had found my own rarity: not from a website, not been told of its location, not been pointed out by other birdwatchers, but all mine! I knew it wasn't a glossy ibis as I remember them being all black, these birds had a black neck and head with off-white flanks and back, and a short black 'tail'. I was scribbling down the identification details when a human competitor, carrying a fishing net and looking for morsels from around the rock pools, came too close and two of the birds took flight revealing more details, the white wings with a black trailing edge and black legs. It was definitely an ibis, but which one? With no computer or bird

115

books I decided to text the details to my son for him to give me a positive identification. Now I had to wait so I decided that we needed a drink in a nearby bar to celebrate my find.

That evening I received a reply from my son starting with that ominous phrase that makes me nervous: "first the good news" - it was definitely a sacred ibis. The bad news was that these birds are the French equivalent of our ring necked parakeets i.e. escapees that are becoming a pest!

Breeding populations of sacred ibis were established in zoological gardens in the 1970s including one in Brittany where the young were allowed to fly free and now wild breeding colonies have been established around the western coast of France, the largest at the mouth of the Loire estuary contained 820 nests. By the time I got home and found a website detailing their spread in France and to other European countries there was also a photograph of four ibises perched on the sides of open rubbish containers at the rear of a McDonalds, my bubble had been well and truly deflated.

I mean, just how many birds breeding in the wild do you need before they can be classified as wild. Now that is something I must look into...

Are Birdwatchers Getting Lazy?
September 2009

After a recent birdwatching trip I found myself wondering if the majority of birdwatchers (and I include myself) want things too easy these days. Do we too easily turn to the hide where we can sit down in relative comfort, be shielded from the elements and perhaps afforded a degree of companionship with like minded people? Do we rely on others too much to find or even identify the birds?

It started with a call from a friend of mine. Five glossy ibises had been present for a couple days at the RSPB reserve at Dungeness and he asked if I wanted to go and see them. Having never seen a glossy ibis I wasn't going to pass up on a chance of a 'lifer', so the next day we set off for Dungeness. We parked the car and stepped out into the near gale force winds blowing across the open shingle landscape and were pleased it was only a short walk to the shelter of the Hanson ARC hide. The hide overlooks a large shallow gravel pit and it was here that the ibises had been seen on occasions over the past few days. Inside were around a dozen other grateful birdwatchers, most no doubt hoping to see an ibis but after a couple of brief conversations we established that the birds had not been seen today. Despite the fare before us, which included seven species of duck, great crested grebes and a large number of cormorants we felt a little disappointed at not seeing the birds, so, after an hour, we left the hide.

Back at the car we had lunch sitting on the ledge of the open hatchback sheltered from the wind. We had just finished our sandwiches when my friend shouted "Ibis!" and pointed straight ahead. We watched the three birds fly low over the willows and were certain they must have landed on the gravel pit. We hurried back towards the hide but not before stopping a car that was just leaving and informing them that we had just seen the ibises; they pulled over and followed us to the hide. Expectantly, we opened the door only to find the inhabitants subdued and not staring intently through their telescopes. We asked if the ibises had flown in as we had seen them and were sure that they must have passed almost over the top of the hide but were met with shaking heads and muttered 'no's but our news did at least appear to get everyone scanning the area with renewed hope. We sat down along with the others who had followed us from the car park and started looking once again. I began to think we had jumped the gun and raised the expectations of a hide full of birdwatchers. Time dragged slowly but after around ten minutes, to our relief, someone at the other end of the hide said "there's one flying left". Although the ibis flew out of view from the hide, at least we felt vindicated. It wasn't long before another voice said "I have one" and gave directions to the rest of the hide and soon we were all watching the bird; to our delight, another glossy ibis appeared as if from nowhere.

We did wonder how three ibises flew into the scrape without a hide full of birdwatchers noticing. But that was not the only bird that I and almost everyone else failed to see. Another birdwatcher had picked out a little stint among a number of dunlin and gave everyone directions and kindly pointed out its distinguishing features. Don't get me wrong I certainly appreciate birds being pointed out to me and lots of birdwatchers can learn from more experienced 'birders but I wonder if a number of us could try harder to find them ourselves. It does take a lot of application to look through a flock of birds in the hope that amongst them there might be another species!

Happy that we had seen the ibises, we left, although somewhat disappointed with their rather dull brown plumage as I was expecting something shinier given their name. We crossed the road and drove along a track to the main car park and the visitors centre. As we entered we noticed that the ibises were not on the sightings board, when we informed them they immediately added them to the list and within minutes four or five other 'birders' standing nearby asked for directions to the Hanson ARC hide.

After a brief look round the shop we decided that we must brave the wind once again and so set off along the track. The wind was strong enough to generate waves on the gravel pits and the reeds were bending almost double with only a few coots trying to find shelter around the edges. We came to another hide with two birdwatchers in it but we did not stay long as the windswept scene was bleak and virtually bird-less with only one grey plover in an acre of mud and a passing crow battling against the wind.

Continuing along the track, we came upon another birdwatcher scanning the leeward side of a belt of small trees, bushes and brambles. He was watching two chiffchaffs flitting back and forth plucking insects from among the branches. The sun was now out and in the shelter of the bushes this spot was apparently warm enough to attract insects. We joined him in watching the birds and also with the hope that if this location was okay for chiffchaffs who knows what else may turn up? The birdwatcher moved on and, as we continued to watch, one or two of the passing birdwatchers would ask what we were looking at but very few bothered to take a look at the chiffchaffs and carried on to the next hide. As it happened we didn't find anything else there or in a couple of similar 'havens' nearby.

I know the wind made birdwatching difficult but I could not help noticing how few observers were spending any time looking apart from in the comfort of the hides. Almost to demonstrate my point the next hide was nearly full but, unfortunately, there was not a lot on view. We got talking to a birdwatcher who informed us that he had heard that tree sparrows had been seen recently on the reserve but he had not seen them himself. So after a blustery walk around a number of other hides, we decided to head back to the centre to see if we could find out more about the sparrows.

Looking at the sightings board it noted that tree sparrows were sometimes seen around the farm buildings situated by the road at the entrance to the reserve so we decided to look for these now rare sparrows on our way out of the reserve. It did not look promising, the wind was tossing back and forth the branches of the few bushes and small trees huddled around the buildings. We stood there searching with our binoculars while traffic on the road to Dungeness flew past us not ten foot away; that, combined with the noise of the wind in the bushes, made listening for any sounds of birds difficult, to say the least. Two or three cars leaving the reserve stopped and the occupants asked us what we were looking for and then promptly left, seemingly not fancying the odds of our success. However, we did hear a couple of faint cheeps and chirps which encouraged us to keep looking. Then - movement in the bushes. It turned out to be a great tit and although it was a handsome individual it was not what we were hoping for. Every now and then we would catch a glimpse of what we were sure were sparrows, but were they tree sparrows? We decided to concentrate on the trees closest to the buildings which afforded some shelter from the wind and it was here that we eventually found our tree sparrow. There were more than one moving around the bush but one individual stayed still long enough to view through our binoculars and even to retrieve the telescope from the car for a closer look. It must be ten years since I have seen a tree sparrow and I had forgotten how clean they look with the black patches on their white cheeks, the black 'bib' and a white collar, and the warm russet-brown cap. What a pity that this resident little bird has suffered a huge decline in numbers in the last twenty five years along with a number of other species linked to farmland mainly due it seems to the intensification of agriculture and the loss of hedgerows.

It was seeing the tree sparrow that gave me the greatest thrill of the day. I suppose it was the feeling that I was watching a bird that was once described as abundant, in my 1965 copy of the Observer's Book of Birds, now hanging on in isolated pockets in the UK and I was surprised that no other birdwatchers looked for it while we were there. Or was it because we had forsaken the comfort of the hide and braved the elements for our sighting?

Most Wanted List
February 2010

I think it started when I retired. Suddenly, having more time to devote to my main interest, wildlife and in particular bird watching, I began to reflect on some of the birds that I have never seen. Why I have now focused on seeing certain birds I am not sure? Maybe it stems from my old Observer's Book of Birds when, as a youngster, I used to gaze at the drawings with their almost mysterious backgrounds giving some species an aura which seemed so exotic to someone restricted to mainly the east end of London. Or maybe they are simply species that I had seen on television or in books and now wish to see in the flesh. Or could it be just the sound of their names?

Whatever the reason, the birds that I have decided to try to find are not particularly rare, after all I am not chasing a gyr falcon or a kentish plover, but I would certainly class them as elusive.The list did include ring ouzel and osprey, I say "did" because a couple of years ago I went to the Peak district and found the ring ouzel in its high rocky domain and a trip to Kent last year yielded a magnificent osprey.

Therefore that now leaves the firecrest and hawfinch as the top two on my most wanted list. So you can imagine why recent reports of up to seven hawfinches having been seen at Lynford Arboretum in Norfolk proved to be irresistible.

The temperature was just above freezing and patches of snow and ice lay in the shaded parts of the arboretum as we pulled into the car park. Armed with information that the birds had been seen in trees around the paddock area on more than one occasion raised our hopes. But where was the 'paddock'? We locked the car and not sure which way to go we asked a passing dog walker if she knew where the paddock was. Her unexpected answer "are you looking for the hawfinches" raised our hopes sky high and she duly gave us directions.

Walking along the woodland path, we noticed a number of small birds moving through the bare trees, with our binoculars and then our telescopes we could see it was a mixed flock of redpolls, goldfinches and siskins, amongst them a particularly striking male redpoll. Alas, no hawfinches.

As we came to edge of the paddock we could see three or four other birdwatchers further along the path but unfortunately they were not staring intently down their telescopes but mainly shifting from foot to foot trying to keep warm. Not the body language of someone watching hawfinches. I suppose it took about an hour to walk around the outside of the paddock stopping at strategic points to scan the surrounding trees or talk to other hawfinch hunters. If the hawfinches turn up then us and at least another six pairs of eyes would surely spot them. In all that time we only had one brief 'incident' but that turned out to be a small flock of redwings.

Determined to try again later, we walked back to the car for lunch and, thankfully, some hot coffee. As is often the case when 'birding', the trees around the car park seemed to have more sounds of birds than the rest of the area so, sandwiches scoffed, we followed our ears. Soon we were watching a flock of siskins flying from tree top to tree top. A short distance on and, to our amazement, a marsh tit flew down into a bare bush not ten feet from us, we didn't even need our binoculars to identify it. Within minutes, flying back and forth around us, were at least three marsh tits, there could have been as many as five but their constant criss-crossing made it difficult to confirm. Then, to add to our delight, a single delicate coal tit searched a close-by bush for any tiny morsels but still no heavy-billed hawfinches so we headed back to the 'paddock'.

On the way, we stopped suddenly as a flock of around a dozen hawfinch sized birds silhouetted against the sky circled the nearby treetops but as soon as they landed and we had them in our telescopes we could see they were crossbills. To see these specialised pine cone feeders with their strange bill that you would think was a hindrance to feeding rather than their means of survival in a rather narrow niche more than made up for our initial disappointment. In addition we were treated to the sight of a male in its red-orange tinged plumage along with a number of the green streaked females.

We carried on back to the paddock and once again birdwatchers had placed themselves at strategic points. If there were any hawfinches around we would have had them well and truly surrounded. Then we noticed some birds in the top of a tree in the centre of the paddock. Was this what we had been looking and hoping for? No, it was those bloody crossbills again. The brief wave of excitement over we went back to conversations with those that had seen them here before which helped to keep our spirits up but after another chilly hour we decided to retreat to the car.

Was I downhearted? How could I be? A day in and around some magnificent trees in the Arboretum with great views of what I would classify as scarce birds and, for good measure, as we walked back to the car, a Muntjac deer passed close to us.

I am sure in time more birds will be added to my list but, in the meantime, if anyone knows of the whereabouts of a hawfinch or a firecrest please get in touch as I will keep looking.

Essex Birds?
March 2010

They are brash, gaudy, raucous and hang around in gangs. No, I am not talking about the often wrongly maligned Essex females but a species of bird that is slowly colonising the South East of England and *is* appearing in Essex in ever increasing numbers.

To see these newcomers a friend and I were given directions which lead us to a pub car park in North Stifford near Grays, not a place I would normally associate with bird watching. From the car park we walked down a sloping grassy field and at a gap in the hedge climbed over a style and came to the bank of the river Mardyke. Along the opposite bank just before the ground started to rise was a belt of mature trees (I think they are white poplars) where, according to the reports, we would find our Essex birds, ring-necked parakeets.

Walking slowly along the riverbank, listening and occasionally scanning with our binoculars the tall, bare trees, with here and there some patches of ivy, we were beginning to think that the reports may have been exaggerated. Then a harsh squawk caught our attention, quickly followed by a glimpse of green in the greyness of the trees which soon had us focussing our binoculars on a ring-necked parakeet. Before long we had picked out around six individuals and were soon marveling at their flamboyant dress and wondering why it took us so long to locate them. Looking through our telescopes we could clearly see the bright green head and chest with a slightly darker green on the wings. In the sunlight, the greens at times seem to take on a yellow hue especially on the feathers under the tail and on the top of the long tails a flash of turquoise could be seen. The typically parrot shaped bill is bright red with a hint of pink and appears to have a matt finish giving the powerful bill an almost 'soft' appearance. And, as if the bird was not colourful enough, the male has a ring around its neck which is black at the front but pink around the nape, hence its alternative name of rose-ringed parakeet.

As we stood there, some individuals flew overhead on pointed wings, calling loudly, as they landed in the trees on our side of the river and by now we reckoned there to be around ten birds showing. Most of these appeared to be in pairs with one or two seemingly inspecting prospective nest holes so the possibility of this colony continuing and even expanding looks promising.

The first records of ring-necked parakeets that were either released or had escaped, establishing breeding colonies in the wild, were in the early 1970s. Now they appear to be spreading out into the countryside from their mainly urban or semi-urban strongholds around Greater London and, depending on the source, estimations of present numbers range from five to ten thousand birds. Their booming population is thought to be partly due to the generosity of us humans in providing food for garden birds helping them survive our winters.

So successful are they, that in 1983 the British Trust for Ornithology added them to the British Birds list under the classification C1 – a naturalised introduced species i.e. the bird is recognised as having a self-sustaining population. Now protected in the wild under the Wildlife and Countryside Act, it is also illegal to release or allow them to escape into the wild. 'Stable door' and 'bolted' come to mind!

Walking away on a chilly day we could not help but admire these colourful birds originally from the much warmer climes of Central Africa or Southern

Asia but introduced into this country as pets and now these British birds are the most northerly breeding population of parrots.

At the moment, the jury is out on whether the growing population of parakeets is adversely affecting our native hole nesting birds such as nuthatch, starlings and woodpeckers, and it is also blamed for damage to buds and blossom on fruit trees.

Let's hope that this 'Essex' bird does not get an undeserved reputation.

A ring-necked parakeet in North Stifford

Blackbird Fight
March 2010

It is not an uncommon sight to see blackbirds in the cold of winter seemingly wasting precious energy on continually chasing other individuals from their 'patch' Most of the time the aggressor successfully sees off the 'rivals' without too much resistance after a short-lived, hopping pursuit.

But one day, as I looked out of our bedroom window, I became witness to an almighty fracas going on below in our neighbour's front garden. The main protagonists were two female blackbirds, facing each other, holding their tails erect, their wings hanging down slightly so the tips of the primaries could be clearly seen below the body.

In the 'wings' there were also two males and a further two females who had minor supporting roles which seemed mainly to consist of squawking encouragement to the main combatants. Part of the action was obscured by shrubs but you could see them dashing two and fro, sometimes spilling out on to the driveway and then hopping or flying back in to the bushes. All the while, they kept up a barrage of 'tchook-tchook-tchook' and 'chink-chink-chink' alarm calls to accompany the rapid flicking of wings. Every so often the two females with thrashing wings would rise slowly, about two feet in the air, all the while clawing and pecking at each other and then crash back down to the ground. After more noisy dashing around by all six birds, the two females would at times lock claws and writhe on the ground, seemingly using their wings to brace or lever themselves to gain some sort of advantage, as if they were engaged in avian greco-roman wrestling. Whether through exhaustion, boredom or victory, the chasing slowed and the scene quietened down as, one by one, the individuals flew off from the arena to nearby roof tops, content now with intermittent cocking of the tail feathers and the odd call. Despite the fury displayed at times, none of the combatants seemed to be harmed. I am just surprised that the commotion did not attract the neighbourhood cats!

At a later date, as I was looking through a field guide, I realized that I may have been mistaken in thinking that the main combatants were females because first year males are also brownish and do not have yellow bills. Young males - I suppose I should have guessed!

Where have all the Aircraft Gone?
April 2010

For around six days in April 2010, large areas of northern Europe became a no-fly zone, due to an ash cloud from a volcanic eruption in Iceland. The volcano Eyjafjallajokull spewed ash into the skies to a height of approximately nine kilometres and caused disruption for hundreds of thousands of would-be air travellers.

At home the effect was eerie, looking up at the sky without the familiar white vapour trails criss-crossing the heavens. At night, the stars had taken centre stage with no winking white or flashing red and green lights from aircraft hurrying to and from numerous points around the globe to distract your gaze. The air seemed stiller as if the planes, in cutting through the atmosphere, somehow created waves or stirred currents that added to the winds. I just stood and listened to the silence. Stillness reigned, even the wind seemed to be taking a rest - not daring to break the calm.

The next morning was lovely and sunny and I could not help but keep on gazing up into the empty, blue, spring sky. No droning of engines; the tranquillity broken only by the cooing of doves and a distant strimmer.

Will I ever know such plane-free days again?

On the morning of the 21st April, it was announced that flights had been resumed. Later that day, two flew over while I was in the garden and I felt that the rumbling growl of the engines was intrusive and the shapes passing overhead were intruding into my personal air space - but I suppose I will just have to get used to it again.

According to Wikipedia, the European flights avoided about 344,109 tonnes of CO_2 emissions per day, while the volcano emitted about 150,000 tonnes of CO_2 per day, so perhaps some good did come of it.

A Patient Hunter
May 2010

On our east facing and rather windy front doorstep we had a pot of narcissus, the variety that has creamy white petals and a yellow-orange centre. While my wife was watering the plants she noticed in among the swaying blooms, on a petal tucked in beside the centre yellow 'trumpet', a spider and called me to look. Unusually, it was white in colour, perfectly camouflaged against the petals and its front legs were stretched wide apart. After consulting my insect book, I found it was in fact a crab spider (Misumena vatia) the female of which can be pale green, white or yellow.

Evidently, crab spiders do not spin webs, but lie in wait on flowers and then ambush any visiting insect. I could not help thinking: did this spider, on finding that it was white, then seek out a white flower in which to hide? If so, that is pretty smart. Or does its pigmentation change to suit whatever flower, within a certain range, it chooses? Either way it would appear that it is not colour-blind. Further investigation on the internet revealed that the spider can change colour within the green/white/yellow band but it does take several days for the chemical changes to take effect. The male is half the size of the female and apparently does not have this range of colouration.

Over the next two or three days I would occasionally take a peek into the flower and see that she was still there. Her position may have changed slightly but her front legs were always wide apart poised ready to pounce on any passing insect. Each time I looked I could not help but admire her optimism, thinking that the chance of a meal must be pretty slim as, apart from the spider, I had never seen any other insect winged or otherwise on or near any of the flowers. Then one day another call from my wife alerted me to a dramatic scene at the pot.. It appeared that the spider had caught a small bee, a honey bee I think, by the head and was greedily sucking the fluids from the body. The spider remained feeding on the bee, which was roughly the same size as itself, for over five hours and during that time the spider had moved the bee around, its jaws now clamped on the abdomen. Later the next day, I looked for the bee and the spider but both had gone.

As the flowers died back I wondered where the white, sideways walking spider had moved to as suitable coloured flowers were not nearby. I imagine that she would show up nicely for any passing bird, an easy target! The hunter becomes the hunted perhaps.

At the end of July my wife brought to my attention another white crab spider this time hiding on a small hibiscus whose flowers consisted of blue petals but with a white stigma. This individual was also a female but unlike the first spider it had faint red lines on either side of the abdomen. Tucked in behind the blue petals, this one was rather obvious but then perhaps they have to compromise from time to time? I am sure it will need all its undoubted patience to surprise its prey this time!

A crab spider feeding on a bee

Creatures of the Night
July 2010

It was a mild evening with only a light wind as I pulled into the car park; perfect conditions I thought for moths, bats and perhaps badgers. I had arrived for one of a series of evening recording sessions being held this year in Marks Hill nature reserve by the Basildon Natural History Society.

Never having attended a recording meeting and only having read about moth traps, I was intrigued to see one in action for the first time especially as it would involve being in woodland in darkness.

As people started to arrive, Brian said he was about to put some food out for the badgers so I tagged along. A walk along the woodland paths brought us to a sett which showed signs of recent digging activity. Brian smeared peanut butter onto some nearby trees at about snout height and we retreated a short distance down the track to watch. As we turned, at the other end of the track a badger was looking at us, his or her facial white flash clear in the gathering gloom, I am sure it must have been watching us as we laid out the treats. Despite the lures, the badger decided not to come any closer but disappeared into the vegetation by the track. As we continued to watch and wait, a song thrush began to sing at the top of its voice seeming even louder in the otherwise tranquil wood. As we watched, another badger(a cub this time) appeared on the track closer to the peanut butter, its black and white striped head tilted upwards as if sniffing the treat or perhaps us. Once again, it disappeared only to reappear a short time later and this time a fox cub joined it on the track. For a few seconds they both stood still looking at us and then melted away.

As the light faded we had no further sightings of badgers but we did have a couple of close encounters with pipistrelles as they flew along the track under the low canopy, hawking for insects just above our heads. Walking back through the woods we saw good numbers of bats in the more open spaces and as we sat on a bench by Peck's pond we were treated to a fine aerial display by, going by size, at least two different species of bats, some passing incredibly close.

By now it was pretty well dark as we made our way through the shadowy wood with various degrees of darkness all around when up ahead we saw two eerie glows and then movement of figures as they changed position in and out of the light. Was it a scene of witchcraft that we had stumbled upon? No, it was moth trapping.

I was really impressed with the operation. A generator was running, supplying power for the two mercury vapour lamps set up about fifty yards apart on different paths in the wood. Below each light was a box with removable, downward sloping lids. At the base of the slope between the lids was a gap of approximately two inches through which you could see that the box was filled with a number of empty egg boxes. The moths attracted to the light would then go down into the box and find shelter amongst the folds of the eggs boxes, or at least that is what I think happens.

The generator also provided power to the 'headquarters' a table with chairs around it and on the table top a raised illuminated magnifying glass and spread out, numerous reference books. Seated around the table were the professionals of the operation, better known as Peter, Rod and Ron, experts in the interrogation of the night-flying insects, determined to discover their identification and numbers.

Other individuals would capture any moths lurking in the boxes under the lights, imprisoning them in small clear plastic specimen jars. They would then take them back to 'headquarters' in batches for identification. It was fascinating to see close up some of these seemingly drab moths reveal their beauty especially when viewed under the magnifying glass and as the night moved on the list of individuals grew longer.

Not all moths were so obliging as to fall headlong into the moth trap but would linger shyly in the shadows of the adjacent vegetation but this did not guarantee their escape as sometimes they would be swept up in what I assume must have been the moth equivalent of a butterfly net. From there, they would be transferred to a specimen jar and then on to the table.

The number of 'prisoners' was mounting and to avoid any confusion it was clear that the system for processing needed to be adhered to. 'New' moths in the jars would be piled on the left of the table and, once identified by the experts, they were placed on the right of the table. Those that did not yield their name, rank or number easily were placed in a separate pile in the centre of the table to be discussed and questioned further by at least two experts. Some specimens who proved to be either difficult to identify, unusual or ornate were often photographed before being moved to the right of the table. As the roll call lengthened I could not help but be intrigued and sometimes amused at some of the names such as; july highflyer, buff footman, maiden's blush, heart and dart, snout and green pug.

With the number of moths mounting, we began to run low on the plastic specimen jars so the process of releasing those that had been positively identified began. The moths were removed from the jars by releasing them into another large cardboard box. I asked the question, "why the cardboard box?" There was a perfectly sensible answer. The moths would be released later at a point away from where we were trapping so as they are not re-trapped and so distort their numbers.

It was not only moths that were on the wing in the hours of darkness, a large longhorn beetle caused quite a stir when brought to the table. It was the first time I had seen one. Also, there were numerous crane flies, bugs and mosquitoes flitting in and around the lights and boxes.

Brian took a few people back to see if the badgers had returned but they remained elusive. And we did keep our ears open in case tawny owls decided to communicate but tonight they remained silent.

I left at around 11.30 pm, soon after the tea and biscuits but others were still busy catching, identifying and counting. By the end of the night's work I was told that one hundred and twenty three individual moths had been identified - belonging to thirty six different species, six of which were new for Marks Hill. Added to the data from past recording sessions the BNHS is beginning to build an important store of knowledge which will form the basis of monitoring the future health and trends of the moth populations and in a way of the wood itself and the environment in general.

I would thoroughly recommend members go along to a recording session and, although there is a serious side to the work, there are also plenty of jokes and laughter throughout the evening. Enjoy a cup of tea and experience nature after dark and maybe add something to your own knowledge. There is room for all levels and if, like me, you mainly just watch, it will still be an adventure.

NB. Don't forget to wear long sleeves, long trousers and you might need insect repellent. Oh! And bring a torch -I forgot!

Wheelie Bin Prison
October 2010

In an effort to reduce the amount of household waste going to landfill Thurrock council have provided its residents with three wheelie bins: a blue one for materials to be recycled, a green one for general household waste and a brown one for food and 'green' garden waste.

The brown bin in particular has proved to be an interesting and useful container. While we already have a compost heap the brown bin does provide an outlet for the more woody cuttings from various shrubs and trees etc. During one of my pruning sessions, I had virtually filled the bin with cuttings. Lifting the lid to add more, I was amazed at the number of insects that were clinging to the underside of the lid or were scuttling around the rim.

Certainly the late summer and autumn pruning would produce green crickets, shield bugs (two varieties), various spiders (including a small green one) and many different ladybirds. Of course these discoveries meant that after each pruning session I would, after an hour or so, have to open the bin to see what had crawled from the cuttings. The trouble is my conscience then dictated that, after having destroyed their peace, I needed to rescue these displaced prisoners and move them to a safe haven within the garden. Seeing the number of insects on the lid, it always surprised me that I never noticed any while I was hacking away at the vegetation! I keep saying that I must arm myself with a specimen container and magnifying glass so that as I fling back the lid I will capture and positively identify the prisoners but for one reason or another I never seem to get round to it. So all you nature lovers: if you have a brown wheelie bin don't forget to have a peek after filling it and release the inmates before consigning them to the compactor vehicle.

However, like most gardeners (I think I just about come into this category) there are certain invertebrates that inhabit our plots that we would like to see the back of and here the brown wheelie bin comes into its own. I often feel squeamish and saddened when killing slugs and snails but now the bin provides the perfect prison to ease my conscience. Over a week you collect the little darlings and place them in the bin feeling that the dark conditions and the vegetation would be ideal for them. While the slugs tend to remain hidden the snails evidently are not that enamoured with the accommodation and often when adding more cuttings or snails you find lots of their brethren clinging to the underside of the lid, obviously trying to escape.

Come the day of the waste collection, the brown bin is lifted on hydraulic grabs, inverted, shaken and returned to the pavement. A quick check in the bin usually reveals one or two determined individuals still adhering to the plastic but most, I like to think, were now heading down the road in the lorry and eventually to the nearest council composting scheme. I think of hundreds of other gardeners doing the same and my imagination runs riot as I see thousands upon thousands of slugs and snails forming huge herds at the landfill site and at dusk moving off in convoy looking for the nearest garden or vegetable plot. Or, if they do what is suggested, will they use their homing instincts and begin the long slink back to our gardens in a very bad mood? Surely the prisoners won't find their way back from there?

In Search of a Firecrest
January 2011

Two years ago, there had been a number of reports of a firecrest in Hockley Woods and some even gave a rough description of where within the wood it was located. Having never seen a firecrest, I was keen to join a friend (who had also heard of the sightings) to search for it. Firecrest: even the name sounds exciting and it is a bird that a number of well known birdwatchers have identified as one of their favourites and I felt it was time to see one for myself. Although others had found the bird, I sensed there was still some personal groundwork to be done. I consulted a number of reference books and a CD for diagnostic features of the bird, its behaviour and even listened to recordings of its call.

From my notes, we arrived at around 12.30 pm and, armed with some basic directions from the website, we scoured the patches of bramble interspersed with holly bushes between the bare mature trees for our 'quarry'. I must admit that when I saw the undergrowth and the size of the area covered by the past sightings the thought of finding a predominantly olive green bird which, along with the goldcrest, is the smallest in Britain, brought 'needle' and 'haystack' to mind.

After approximately an hour, we had slowly covered most of the area where the bird had been seen but with no luck. During that time I had heard the calls of numerous blue tits, great tits and robins, sometimes all at once, so by now I had completely forgotten the call of the firecrest from the CD. Even if I had remembered it, I doubt if I would have had the confidence or skill to recognise it from the various intermittent background calls, including high pitched 'zits', 'chinks' and whistles. Sometimes our imaginations got the better of us and a blue tit seen out of the corner of the eye became a possible firecrest. In fact after another hour of patiently searching even a flash of movement from a squirrel in the shadows made me think 'is that it?'.

A conversation with another birdwatcher who had seen it only the day before confirmed that for the last two hours we had at least been looking in the right area. He did point out the exact location he had seen it so, ever optimistic, we looked - but without success.

The good thing about seeing numerous blue tits and great tits is that you do get your 'eye in' and when we saw something different, smaller, and of uniform colour flit from a holly bush into nearby bramble it stood out and the excitement mounted. We quietly made our way to where the bird flew and managed to get a few quick glimpses as it flitted in and out of the low bramble, often in shadow. Being almost continuously on the move, disappearing then reappearing, I could not get my binoculars on it; my friend was luckier and was able to see the firecrest's diagnostic white stripe over the eyes. The bird disappeared into the bramble and despite another twenty minutes or so searching we could not relocate it and therefore we decided to call it a day and adjourned to the nearby 'Bull' to reflect on events over a pint.

So, although I had now finally 'seen' a firecrest I felt disappointed that the view I had did not allow me to see the distinguishing marks of this tiny bird. Consequently, I wondered if I should really count it at all; and so, if the bird remained, it was likely I would be back to Hockley woods for another try.

Over the next two years we returned to Hockley Woods in the winter but without success. On occasion, just to rub salt in the wound, there would inevitably be a report on the website of a male singing from a holly bush or two birds seen together. Grrrr! If fact, we also visited two or three other sites in Essex and Norfolk where the firecrest had been reported but with the same outcome. Of course, these trips were still enjoyable as there were always other birds to see and the ever-changing countryside to wander in.

In January 2011 we decided on another visit to Hockley Woods - this time hoping to see lesser spotted woodpecker and nuthatch. We had a good day seeing a stock dove, a small flock of lesser redpolls with two or three siskins amongst them and (as hoped) a nuthatch and a lesser spotted woodpecker, a bird that is becoming increasingly rare. As we arrived back at the car park, we met another birdwatcher who had seen a firecrest only fifteen minutes ago and pointed to the area. To cover the spot, we split up and slowly searched the nearby holly bushes. As I moved around a bush, I did hear some faint high pitched 'tweets' from within and then a sighting of a very small bird. Straining my eyes, I had a few more brief glimpses of the energetic bird as it searched for morsels but I was still unable to get a definitive view. As the bird disappeared once again I was starting to think that I would not be able to positively identify it. Then, as I tried to locate the bird it suddenly appeared in a gap between the leaves and I saw my first firecrest. No doubts, no 'might be', it could only be a firecrest. Funnily enough, it was not the delightful multi striped head that impressed me the most, it was the bronze-orange patch on the shoulder which seemed to have an almost metallic sheen to it. In the meantime, I had managed to alert my friend and we both tried to follow the bird when it flew to another nearby patch of holly. Once again, it required patience and luck to catch a good view of this energetic bird and we continued to watch its relentless probing until it finally disappeared from view.

So, finally, I have really seen a firecrest. Now I appreciate why birdwatchers like to see this pretty little bird. Over the following couple of weeks, other birdwatchers reported seeing the firecrest almost daily and it amazed me how all the sightings were concentrated in the same small area. Had the bird found a productive location and was not keen to leave it, or were there a number of them?

A sketch of a hawfinch

Hawfinch Quest
February 2011

Ever since I acquired a copy of the Observers' Book of Birds way back in my 'formative years' I have always been fascinated by the hawfinch and especially the description of its bill: "powerful enough to crack fruit stones" it read. Even in East London I had been well acquainted with the other common 'finches' but the hawfinch remained elusive and mysterious. Now in retirement, with more time at my disposal I have been actively following up, unsuccessfully so far, on sightings of hawfinches.

After last year's chilly failures to see a hawfinch which took me as far afield as Norfolk, I looked forward to more opportunities in 2011 to find the shy coccothraustes coccothraustes (hawfinch) but the year did not start successfully.

In late January after reports of hawfinches being seen on two or three consecutive days in Braxted Park, Essex we decided to have a look. Unfortunately, on the day we chose, the birds decided not to put in an appearance - leaving us and around five other birdwatchers with time to reminisce about past 'birding' successes or failures while stamping our feet as we stood in the cold wind. Although disappointing, the day was not without its interest as we did see three buzzards and a red kite, two species that not too many years ago you would have been unlikely to see in Essex. But it was the hawfinch, a bird I have never seen, that I really wanted to find. Then, to add insult to injury, after our visit, the birds were reported on most of the following days with numbers reaching up to twenty!

Hawfinches seem to melt away into the countryside in summer and only in winter, when they gather in groups among the bare trees do birdwatchers have a reasonable chance to admire this large secretive finch. We wonder what conditions or surroundings attract flocks of hawfinches to particular spots where they do seem to return again and again. So, we had to brave the winter weather once again and return to the same location.

Therefore, in early February, with painful memories of the four hours spent in near freezing conditions still fresh in my mind, I once again started to gather together my birdwatching paraphernalia in preparation for a return visit to Braxted the following morning. On arrival, we parked the car in the same spot as the previous week and walked up the same footpath with our fingers crossed. Within a hundred yards we could see up ahead two other birdwatchers in conversation but unfortunately not looking through their telescopes or binoculars. We stopped and surveyed the surrounding tree tops but apart from a few blue tits and long tailed tits it seemed quiet. Then, after a short while, my friend said "I think I have them". I swung round to see where he was looking and trained my binoculars on a small flock of birds high in the tree tops. Right size, right colouration, they were definitely hawfinches. Now my panic started to set in as they were a long way off and as I was frantically extending the legs of my telescope to get a better view some started to move off. I could imagine this fleeting glimpse being all I would get. After what seemed ages, I managed to focus the telescope on my first hawfinch. I could not believe it - it had its back to me! Thankfully, as they moved along the branches some turned towards me and then at last I had a view of that magnificent heavyweight bill.

The other two birdwatchers had seen our intense activity and quickly joined us in viewing an estimated ten birds. They appeared to be feeding on the buds of an oak tree but soon moved to another nearby tree and it was here that I had my finest view of a male bird and I was not disappointed. The massive bill, ivory in colour, as impressive as any illustration or photograph I had ever seen, the chestnut cap, black bib and even the unusual blue-black twisted secondaries that look like a line of small triangles were visible.

One by one they started to move down the line of trees and out of our view. I could not believe it; we had been there less than an hour and I had finally seen not one but ten hawfinches. As we walked back towards the car two other birdwatchers arrived and asked had we seen the hawfinches. Thankfully we were able to say "yes".

Feeding the Birds?
February 2011

Like many others I have a number of feeders filled
with nuts and seeds, some with multiple perches,
all to draw in and accommodate our feathered
friends. They alight on the feeders or await their
turn in the nearby bare bushes, the impatient or
hungry sometimes scrapping with others to secure a
space on the feeders. The consequence of these
concentrations of birds, especially in the harsher
winter months, is not that unexpected. It is bound
to attract the attention of a sparrowhawk.

Its presence is often betrayed by the behaviour of
other birds; whether it is the panicked 'cracking'
wings of the collared doves as they scatter or the
starlings flying high and forming a flock to shadow
the raptor overhead. Sometimes it is the alarm calls
that can be heard or sometimes the birds all go
quiet.

Despite these defence mechanisms, the
preferred method of attack is still to use the
element of surprise and I have often seen the bird
hurtle through the garden at head height, past the
feeders and away through a gap in the bushes.
Sometimes these tactics nearly pay off and the
hawk brakes, twists and turns in pursuit of the
fleeing birds. On one occasion I heard the sound of
fluttering wings and the crashing of branches and
looked to see a sparrowhawk in a neighbour's tree
regaining its balance and composure after what I
can only think was an unsuccessful attack. A couple
of shakes of her head and wings and she was off,
empty-handed.

But obviously the tactics must be successful for
the hawk to survive and, although I have never seen
an actual 'hit', I have seen a female sparrowhawk

plucking and eating a collared dove on the lawn and an immature female pinning a blackbird to the ground before flying off with it in her talons. On other occasions I have found piles of feathers that would seem to point to a sticky end for the owner.

So it was not a complete surprise when I recently looked out the kitchen window to see a male sparrowhawk on the garden wall tearing at a motionless house sparrow that it held in its claws. I have never seen a male this close before and I could see its powder blue/grey back, the delicate orangey barring on the breast concentrated along its flanks and cheeks, its powerful yellow legs and piercing stare. As it fed, it was constantly alert, looking around for any signs of danger. What did surprise me was that after much pulling and ripping it ate both legs, swallowing them claw first. It took around twenty five minutes to completely finish the meal, whereupon it flew to the nearby apple tree and wiped its hooked beak on the branches. Then, as if it was digesting its meal it sat there quietly, upright, for around ten minutes before flying off.

I did look on the ground either side of the wall to see if I could find any remains but amazingly there was nothing apart from a few small feathers, no waste at all!

As I reflected on the events that had taken place not ten foot from a feeder, I could not help but think that this put the notion of feeding the birds in a different light. Only that morning I had topped up the feeders and spread seed on the ground but I like to imagine that by helping birds to survive the winter weather its means more are available for predation. A balance perhaps?

In Search of Cirl Buntings
March 2011

Over the last few years, I have made an effort to seek out birds that I have never seen before. I finally succeeded with ring ouzel, merlin, osprey and 2011 has started well with both firecrest and hawfinch 'ticked' off during the winter. So, fresh from those successes, I thought I would concentrate on finding two other species this year - the cirl bunting and the golden oriole. As the golden oriole would not be returning to these shores until May, the resident cirl bunting was the obvious first target.

Now this presented a problem. The bird is at the northern limit of its range in the UK and my only hope of seeing them was to visit Devon, their last stronghold. Therefore I had to convince my wife that Devon would be lovely in late March. With the prospect of seeing some spring flowers, a favourable weather forecast and a nice hotel she agreed. But where in Devon? A friend gave me a birdwatching magazine which mentioned a couple of possible locations. The magazine also gave the website for the Devon Bird Watching and Preservation Society (DBWPS) which had details of a winter feeding station for cirl buntings. A quick email to the site asking for directions and any other locations and the next day I had further information and two other places to try. At the feeding station they stopped feeding them by mid-March but I was advised to take my own packet of budgie seed and they would very likely turn up. Another email detailed exactly where the birds were fed – at the back of the second car park by the large willow beside the gate that led into an arable field. I then looked it up using online maps and could see the actual tree and gate from the satellite image. Amazing but it all felt too easy! Perhaps to ease my conscience I perused as many books, photographs and articles on cirl buntings to ensure that I could differentiate between them and yellowhammers, especially the females. I even listened to recordings of their calls just in case they had dispersed and the males might be heard singing to establish territories.

After a five hour drive, we arrived in a warm and sunny Brixham and settled into our hotel. The next morning after a quick check of the map we set off for nearby Broadsands. As we neared our destination, those satellite images came to life and I knew exactly where to go. We parked the car and walked to the barred off back car park as per our directions, my pace quickening as we neared the spot. In front of us was the hedgerow which separated the car park from the steeply rising fields beyond and we could see the open wooden gate beside the large willow.

I set up the telescope, placed my rucksack on the ground and took out the budgie seed. Where did I spread the seed? Now, I had to think for myself. Apart from the vehicle tracks leading through the gate the grass was too long, so I threw a couple of handfuls onto the tracks. I then walked around the front of the willow where the lower branches overhung the rough stony ground at the edge of the car park. There, I saw piles of wind-blown empty seed husks caught in the crumbling surface; evidence of the winter feeding. I had found the answer to my question - it was necessary to lay the seed in the open at the edge of the car park! I threw a few handfuls of seed around with perhaps an exaggerated swing of my arm (just in case they were watching from a distance!)

Retreating back to the telescope around fifty feet from the seed, we waited....

Movement in the hedgerow caught our attention but it turned out to be a chiffchaff flitting in and out of sight. Then two birds landed on the seeded area but through the binoculars we could see that they were dunnocks. Our attention was temporarily diverted by a buzzard in the top of a tree on the brow of the hill surveying the ground and another was circling high in the sky. When we looked back to the willow there were more birds on the ground and this time one was a female cirl bunting. By the time I had focussed the telescope there were now two females and a male each slowly and methodically crushing the tiny seeds in their bills. This deliberate feeding meant that they remained comparatively still and they afforded us fantastic views. Then, to our delight, more buntings flew down and at one point we had four males and five females all feeding at once and all adopting the same rather crouched posture. The males (and one in particular) were resplendent with their yellow and black striped heads, an olive green breast band and chestnut on the shoulders. The females lack the yellow and black but do have a distinctive stripe above the eye and delicate brown streaking on the breast and belly.

It was a privilege watching these lovely delicate little birds which are clinging on in these outposts here in South Devon. Winter feeding stations such as this are one of the conservation efforts to maintain their numbers, while measures to try to introduce more sensitive farming practices are pursued.

After around thirty minutes, another two birdwatchers armed with more budgie seed joined us; so there we were: four birdwatchers standing in the middle of an empty car park. I suppose the occasional passer-by had seen this strange behaviour throughout the winter and thought no more about it. I am pleased to say that occasionally all the buntings would suddenly disappear into the hedge or willow when a passing dog walker or something else spooked them. It demonstrated that despite being fed by humans they still retained all the instincts of wild birds. When they judged that the danger had passed they would return one by one to the feast spread on the ground.

As we left, I don't know why but I couldn't help feeling a little guilty as it seemed the birds were laid on a plate for me. After all, we only had to wait for around ten minutes after distributing the seed when they started to appear. I decided that the next day we would visit another location where they have been seen (Berry Head) but after two or three hours searching in what looked like ideal habitat we never saw or heard one. Ah well, we did try. So, I have finally seen a cirl bunting and what a handsome bird it was. Now for the golden oriole!

A Golden Chance?
May 2011

Points on identification - checked; behaviour - checked; habitat - checked; calls and the timing of their arrival - all had been checked. It was early May and the weather forecast looked favourable. Our bags were packed and the alarm set for five a.m. for an early getaway in an attempt to see a rare exotic visitor to our shores.

After a few unforeseen delays on the journey we arrived at the RSPB's Lakenheath Fen reserve in Suffolk at around 8 am, later than ideal, but the wind still seemed light so perhaps we were not too late. Outside the still-closed visitors' centre we took a leaflet from the information board which had a map of the reserve and looked for the locations of the poplar plantations this bird frequents.

Walking past the low scrub and reedbeds towards the plantations we could hear numerous whitethroats, reed warblers and an occasional grasshopper warbler but I felt compelled to reach the trees rather than lingering to seek out these smaller summer visitors.

Talking to other birdwatchers returning from the stands of poplars they reported that they had heard the bird calling earlier but it had remained elusive. However, they still gave us directions as to where they last heard it. Further on, we met another two birdwatchers chatting but not looking through their optics, they had not seen or heard the bird and after exchanging pleasantries we again moved on.

As we approached an area where two more birdwatchers were standing, our casual conversation was abruptly halted by a short fluting, haunting call that you could almost imagine hearing in a tropical rain forest. It was, unmistakably, a male golden oriole (Oriolus oriolus). All ears and eyes were now strained on the trees where we thought the call was emanating.

This bright yellow and black male, the size of a blackbird, with a red bill, who had flown thousands of perilous miles from Africa and had once again, returned to this plantation in the hope that his voice will attract a female who just might have made the identical arduous journey to the same woodland.

The voice moved and the birdwatchers moved, our heads turning like radar tracking stations trying to pinpoint a signal from space. By now there must have been around ten birdwatchers all focused on a relatively small area of poplars in regimented rows, all speaking in hushed tones so as not to miss the next rich notes. Within a short time, birdwatchers were stationed on footpaths to the north, south and east of the woodland where the calls were coming from. We had the bird almost surrounded! Not only were we staring at the shivering leaves but also at the other birdwatchers looking for signs of anybody actually sighting the bird. However, despite its colourful plumage it remained invisible amongst the green leaves.

We probably spent around an hour and half trying, wishing, hoping for even the briefest of glimpse of this exotic bird. At one point we thought it was either throwing its voice or there was more than bird: but it was not to be, the calls became less frequent and then the bird fell silent or had moved elsewhere. And no one saw it!

We were left to talk amongst ourselves, some were regulars to the reserve in the search for golden orioles and told us of times past when the numbers of birds were higher and sightings were more commonplace. Evidently, in recent years the numbers had dwindled and last year it was thought that only one male arrived and, sadly, despite his persistent singing no female was seen.

The few remaining breeding pairs of golden orioles in the UK are now virtually confined to East Anglia where they frequent the remnant plantations of hybrid black poplars. These trees were originally planted mainly for the matchstick industry or as shelter belts on the fens, many have since been felled or have deteriorated due to old age. The RSPB is trying to encourage replanting and have planted some new stands on the Lakenheath reserve. Whether they will be successful in attracting more breeding pairs is difficult to forecast as the golden oriole is at the northern limit of its breeding range in the UK and therefore it is likely that it will always struggle to establish itself here.

As I came away from the reserve I could not help but admire nature in its ability to draw my wife and I out of bed at some unearthly hour, drive for two hours, then spend another two or three mainly gazing at uniform foliage, being occasionally teased by a beautiful sound from a handsome unseen bird and yet we know we will be back next year.

N.B Looking in my old 'Observer's Book of Birds' it describes the call as a clear, fluty, challenging 'Who are you-oo?' Kind of sums it up, I think.

A sketch of a golden oriole

Elephant Hawkmoth
September 2011

It was towards the end of September and I was standing on my front doorstep idly surveying the street. I don't know what made me take a second look at what I initially thought was a curled up leaf. It was on the ground between the wheelie bins on our drive and I was glad I did, for I could see now that it was definitely moving. It was a very large, brownish caterpillar and, even with my limited knowledge, I knew that at around two and a half inches long it must be one of the hawkmoths but which one? It had to be captured for identification purposes so I grabbed the dustpan! Perhaps not the best thing but it was at hand and it worked. The beast walked in and I was able to lift it to eye level for a closer look. The head was rather bulbous with what looked like two pairs of large eyes on either side but as I was studying the markings it slowly extended a 'snout'. Now I could see more markings that looked like another set of smaller eyes further along the 'snout' and the rather small head resembled a nose. In fact, as it started to move again, my initial thoughts were that the head, now extended, looked like the head of a miniature mouse or shrew. I had to get some photographs of this creature so now, armed with my digital camera and insect reference book, it did not take long to identify it as the larva of the elephant hawkmoth. Of course, now I could see why it's called an elephant hawkmoth, I had not really thought about it before.

On reflection, perhaps my own observation was not so far out, after all I am sure I read somewhere that the mouse or shrew is related (albeit distantly) to the elephant. Or am I getting confused with elephants being frightened of mice?

I can't remember seeing the larva of an elephant hawkmoth before and what happened four days later, you guessed it - I saw another! Or was it the same one? This one was about to walk into the road when our next door neighbour's daughter spotted it and called me. As I picked it up it quickly retracted its snout and as it lay in the palm of my hand it periodically convulsed its body, all part of its defence mechanism. I carried it round to my back garden and released it close to where I left the earlier one.

Looking on the internet, I saw that these caterpillars are often found feeding on fuchsia leaves and my neighbours have two large specimens in their front garden so maybe that's where they came from. If that is the case, I wonder why they had abandoned the bushes for the open road?

Elephant hawkmoth caterpillar

New Year, New List, New Telescope
February 2012

Like numerous other birdwatchers, I keep a list of birds that I see during a year. Although I would never consider myself a serious 'lister', having never achieved even the hundred and fifty mark. Unfortunately, my record keeping does not help. It is a bit haphazard with the result that, come the end of the year, I often look back on some glaring omissions. Surely I must have seen a cormorant or a lapwing or a linnet? While the rarer ones are eagerly noted, the more mundane can easily slip through the net. Now, six weeks into 2012, my modest year list is slowly growing.

One interesting addition in January was a noisy male ring-necked parakeet which amazingly turned up in my garden on three consecutive days. This exotic bright green bird with its elegant long tail seemed somewhat out of place against the sombre greys of winter, nimbly feeding on the peanut feeder, but its successful expansion in England means it is now established on the British Bird list and therefore can be included on my list.

Now in early February, after a number of almost daily reports of a jack snipe in Southchurch Park East, a friend and I thought we would try our luck. After the heavy snowfalls over Eastern England three days earlier, the main roads were now clear but the side roads around the park were still covered in compacted snow and ice. It had been many years since I took my son to play hockey in Southchurch Park but I could vaguely remember a small lake at the eastern end of the park. My memory did not let me down. The ice crunched under our wheels as we pulled into the frozen, snow covered car park, close to the lake. It was still around zero degrees as we quickly put on boots, hat and gloves and with telescopes over our shoulders we crunched our way across the snow towards the water. It was only around 9 a.m. and the winter sun was still low in the sky, casting a shadow over half the lake. The lake was in the middle of a field and bordered on two sides by housing, on the other by a road and lastly a school playing field; not exactly a wild vista. Large areas of the lake were covered in ice, concentrating the collection of ducks and a few little grebes in the open areas. We got talking to a man holding a bag of bread and he mentioned that while feeding the ducks a water rail had joined in for a portion of the largesse. We soon realised that he was very knowledgeable about birds and was able to tell us what had been seen where on the lake, including the jack snipe. After that conversation, my hopes of seeing a jack snipe for the first time were raised another notch.

We soon found a water rail, stalking purposefully along the edge of the grey-brown husky reeds with its long red bill showing well. Then, among the sparse vegetation on the opposite bank, bathed in the morning sun, I found a snoozing snipe-coloured wader. Unfortunately. it was only a common snipe, no matter how many times I tried to make the case for a jack snipe. I wandered further along the lake for a view into the far corner when I heard a shout, I looked round to see my friend frantically beckoning me. Clumping through the snow, ensuring I did not slip, with my precious new telescope gripped firmly, I made my way back. "It's here" he said and let me look through his scope and sure enough there it was, my first sighting of a jack snipe (Lymnocryptes minimus). I quickly set up my scope and found the bird, and then while we were both watching it started to 'bounce', a gentle rhythmical up and down motion of the body while seemingly on static legs. All the books describe this diagnostic movement and now here I was witnessing it firsthand. The bird was noticeably smaller than a snipe; in fact, in 'Birds Britannica' it states that wildfowlers used to call it the 'half snipe'. Its plumage is a mixture of warm browns, buff and black with a bold buff stripe above the eye and two larger buff stripes on each side of the body. We watched it as it moved slowly behind the dead reeds, emerging from time to time, sometimes stopping to give a short 'bobbing' performance, before it eventually disappeared behind a long discarded car tyre, half submerged among the reeds at the water's edge.

Water rail, snipe and jack snipe - three delightful birds, all on a small lake in a park surrounded by houses. Yet without optics they would have been difficult to see and likely to have gone undetected. I did wonder if I had invested too much money in my new telescope but when I think of the clarity of the images I had of that shy winter visitor with the long bill, I felt somewhat justified.

On the basis of further reported sightings we moved on to another nearby park, Friars Park, where mandarin ducks had been seen. Negotiating more icy surfaces on car parks and footpaths, we thankfully arrived upright at the lake. We scanned the water with our binoculars. Plenty of mallards and other species but not what we were looking for. Then, something 'different' in the over hanging vegetation caught my eye so we walked on around the lake to get a better view. It turned out to be a female red-crested pochard but as we focused in we noticed further back in the shadows of the bank-side bushes an altogether more spectacular duck. There were in fact three male mandarin ducks quietly hiding their glamorous attire from the bright, snow-reflected light. I could not begin to describe the intricacies of the patterns and colouring these males display, much better to just look at a photograph. According to 'Birds Britannica' there is now an expanding population of around seven thousand of these birds which have their stronghold in the Home Counties. Both the red crested pochard and the mandarin duck are now included on the British List as naturalised established species and naturalised introduced species respectively. Therefore, the two ducks, the two snipes and the water rail have added five more species to my 2012 tally.

After our early successes our hopes were high for some interesting sightings from Southend pier but after paying £3 to park on the seafront and walking the short distance to the pier entrance we were confronted with a notice informing us the pier was closed due to icy conditions! Determined not to completely waste our £3 we sat on a seafront bench in the sunshine to eat our sandwiches. In front of us, searching for food, along the last narrow ribbon of uncovered beach, were a number of busy sanderlings and turnstones. Further out, a few gulls were quietly floating on the calm water. This tranquil scene was interrupted on the opening of our sandwich boxes. More gulls came in, including a mediterranean gull (another one for the list), and either settled closer in on the water or wheeled overhead. Feral pigeons appeared from nowhere and, when we dispersed a few crumbs, even the turnstones took the opportunity of a snack. The turnstones were so close that there was no need for binoculars, let alone my new telescope!

Am I right in thinking that over the last twenty years turnstones have become tamer, or is it just my imagination? So, if you need turnstone for your year list I can recommend Southend seafront at high tide - but bring some bread just in case.

Harbingers of Spring
March 2012

As the signs of spring gather pace, the phrase 'harbinger of spring' comes to mind. But what does the word harbinger mean? Looking in the Concise Oxford English Dictionary, it was a word once used for an advance company of an army sent ahead to prepare a camping ground. It could also be a pioneer, a forerunner, or to announce or presage.

In fact, I think it is a perfect word to describe nature's signs of transition, from the dormant, iron grip of winter, to the awakenings and promise of spring.

Each year I look forward to these harbingers of gentler times and I often ask myself the question, if I had to choose just one which captures most completely that sense of anticipation or renewal, what would it be?

Being a birdwatcher, I naturally assumed it would likely be an avian event such as the black headed gulls regaining their chocolate brown heads or the elevated song of a skylark heralding another mating season or the arrival of the early migrants such as wheatears or sand martins. In fact, while writing this piece I went outside to the garden on March 26th and, unbelievably, that quintessential harbinger, the swallow, appeared over the garden. A male with a majestically long forked tail, my earliest bird ever, nearing the end of his journey in a search for a breeding site; perhaps the same site as last year!

Or maybe it is the yellow catkins of the pussy willow that makes you think of warmer times ahead, as the awakening, winged insects look to the plant as a vital source of early nectar?

Then, I recall walking through woodland and seeing colourful patches of wonderful flowers such as wood anemones, primrose or lesser celandine, all flowering in a rush to beat the shading of the light by the foliage of the trees. Or is it the sight of those magnificent 'floating' carpets of bluebells on Langdon Hills?

Each year in the garden, I marvel at the sudden synchronised arrival of frogs into my pond and wonder where they have been hiding all winter. Their croaking in the darkness and their brief passionate fling, leaving behind their progeny encased in 'jelly'. Further afield, perhaps it is the sight of a sluggish adder, newly enticed from its subterranean nest, lying quietly coiled in the sun, slowly warming its sinews.

Or, if you are really lucky, perhaps its the spectacle of hormone- fuelled 'mad' March hares dashing around or even boxing on the flat, open spaces of Fobbing Marsh that makes you think of spring.

As much as all these wonderful events do herald the coming of spring, my favourite harbinger is the brimstone butterfly. To glimpse this delicate pastel-yellow butterfly (especially the deeper, brighter male) flitting past the dark stands of leafless blackthorn in the early spring sunshine is to me a marvelous sight of coming regeneration and promise. To think this creature, without fur or feather, has survived as an adult, the snow and freezing temperatures and has emerged on the rise of the ambient temperature. I saw one this year on February 23rd.

Of course, whatever your favourite, it will most likely depend on that enormous glowing orb in the sky. The sun and the orbit of the earth control the seasons, the day length and of course the temperatures on the earth which in turn triggers all of our harbingers.

There must be countless choices but what is your favourite harbinger of spring?

Moving In
April 2012

Over the past few days I have noticed a pair of great tits inspecting a desirable, detached residence in my garden. This keen interest seems to have annoyed the local house sparrows, for after seemingly finding the entrance hole too narrow in the past, they have now started peering in and standing on the roof! However, the great tits stood their ground and, having completed an internal survey, they have decided to move in.

Today, I have been watching them carry beak-fulls of green moss into the nest-box which is attached to the trunk of a gingko tree. I then started to wonder if this chore was a shared responsibility which gave me the task of differentiating between the male and female. The greens and yellow of the male are brighter and he has a much broader black breast stripe that becomes even wider between the legs.

Having established this, it soon became evident that this was an unequal distribution of labour. It was always the female that repeatedly appeared, perching on an adjacent branch, to check the coast was clear before disappearing into the box with the soft green moss in her bill. This is not to say that the male was completely redundant. He appeared to be taking a more supervisory role with occasional 'teach-er, teach-er' calls from nearby vantage points perhaps to announce his territory or as an encouragement to the female's efforts. In addition, I did see him on a couple of occasions with a juicy grub in his bill and the female nearby but, despite carrying the tit-bit from branch to branch and sometimes approaching close to the nest box, he ended up eating it himself. The romantic in me thought that these might be signals to the female that he would be able to provide for their forthcoming offspring!

By late afternoon the cargoes of moss had stopped. Not that the woman's work was done, merely that the base of the nest had been completed and now the material that was being transported to the box had changed. I am not sure what it was but it was white in colour and looked like fine fur or hair, it was obvious that the nest was being lined. Once again frequent trips ensued with one ball of soft hair so large that I wondered if it somewhat obscured her vision in flight! All this hard work was interspersed with stop offs to my seed feeder for re-fuelling and of course the male joined in at these moments.

Later, whether through tiredness or that the job was completed the birds disappeared from view and over the next few days I only saw them on the feeders. I will certainly be monitoring future events with interest.

P.S. The house sparrows obviously have different domestic arrangements as over the past couple of days I have frequently seen a male stripping the soft lining from a hanging basket outside the back door and flying back to a nest box in the garden next door. But then its Latin name is Passer domesticus!

P.P.S Unfortunately, in late autumn when I cleaned out the nest-box I found the skeletons of five young great tits. Not surprising really, after the wet spring and summer, sadly, food must have in short supply.

Flying Tonight
April 2012

The light was just beginning to fade as we gathered for an Essex Wildlife Trust bat evening at the Langdon Hills nature reserve. In the visitors centre around fifteen interested souls were soon listening to the leaders briefing for the evening's escapade. To help us to get a feeling for the weight of the bats we were given three small packages weighing approximately 5g (pipistrelle), 10g (Daubenton's) and largest of all 30g (noctule). A number had brought their own bat detectors and had obviously attended such meetings before but for others, such as myself, the EWT had detectors that after some brief instructions, we could use.

After tea, coffee and biscuits (how civilised), we trooped out into the gathering gloom armed with torches and with detectors at the ready. Thankfully, after the wind and rain of recent days, the evening was dry, still and by comparison of late, mild; the stage was set for a successful evening.

We had only walked about a hundred yards and had just entered an area with trees either side of the path when the first urgent, rapid clicking on a number of detectors could be heard. We had found our first bat (or was that bats?) of the night! The group stopped and were pointing the detectors in all directions and you could hear a barrage of clicks from the line of detectors. At times it seemed the clicking would start at one end of our line and as the bat flew past the clicking would move to other detectors along our line. Although we could 'hear' the bats, seeing them was another thing and, with the trees around us, it was now quite dark but as our eyes became adjusted to the conditions we did manage glimpses of these fast, erratic, flying mammals.

Moving on to the lake, we positioned ourselves on the bank looking out across the still water and in the sky towards the west, the last ribbon of the fading daylight. You could hear the nocturnal honks and quacks of the geese and ducks and see their dark silhouettes gliding along on the far side of the water.

It was not long before the bats were running the gauntlet of our detectors, bringing them to life with hurried click-click-clicks, as they passed in their jerky flight. Once again, despite the numerous audio warnings of their approach, it was not easy to see them and we did wonder just how many bats were around. Some tried shining a torch across the water hoping to pick out a bat skimming the surface hunting for insects but this was largely unsuccessful. We had been there for around forty five minutes when slowly, perhaps coinciding with the dropping temperature, our detectors eventually fell silent.

As we made our way back, now using the torches to aid our progress, a few detectors clicked away as we walked between the trees where perhaps the shelter provided by the trees meant that winged food could still be found. After the recent run of poor weather, I imagine that the bats would need to make the most of the kinder conditions and to continue to feed for as long as possible.

Bats hunt by using echolocation - that is, they emit a high pitched call that bounces back off their prey. To distinguish between some species, it is necessary to know the frequency of their calls and to set your set detector to that frequency (e.g. the call of the lesser horseshoe bat is at 110 kHz). Scientists have recently recognised the soprano pipistrelle as a separate species to the common pipistrelle. It can only be reliably told apart from the common pipistrelle by its echolocation call which is on 55 kHz rather than 45kHz and some members of the group successfully identified a couple of sopranos this evening by having their detectors set at 55kHz.

Most of the bats were identified as pipistrelles but we did think we saw one Daubenton's bat over the lake, taking into consideration its flight pattern, size and its liking for hunting near water.

Safely back at the centre, there was one more treat in store for us. We were introduced to Irwin! Irwin was a live pipistrelle bat that was in the care of the EWT after being nursed back to health and was shortly to be returned to the wild. I was amazed at just how small he was, probably only two inches from snout to hind legs. His folded wing were almost completely hidden under the soft, warm brown fur and you could see his tiny delicate hind claws as he tried to move while being held gently. Was this really the creature we had just seen flashing through the darkness?

Before this evening, I was thinking of purchasing a bat detector and it was a good opportunity to talk to others with experience and see what types they were using. I was hoping that there was one that I had only to point at a bat and it would tell me which species it was. Guess what: it is not as simple as that! A fair bit of skill, knowledge and software is needed to pinpoint a species. So I think I will opt for a fairly simple model!

On my return home I was just locking the car when what did I see fly past a nearby streetlamp? Yep, a bat!

Once in a Lifetime?
September 2012

During September 2012, Rainham Marshes had a very rare visitor. Birdwatchers from all over the UK flocked to the reserve hoping for a glimpse. At the weekends the RSPB opened the gates at 05.00 and extended the closing time to give the travelling birders an improved chance of a tantalising sight of this elusive bird. They even provided a Portaloo close to the hide for their convenience during the times of extended vigils.

The cause of all this excitement was the arrival of a Baillon's crake. According to 'Birds Britannica' there have been only thirteen occurrences in the UK in the last fifty years. Now one has turned up in a patch of sedge just outside a large modern hide.

Surely there would not be a better chance of my seeing one?

It was a bird I have heard of but had merely skimmed over when looking through reference books. After all, my books usually gave it very little space due to its rarity. Now, with the prospect of seeing one, I closely examined the information I did have. What surprised me was its size. It is only a little larger than a house sparrow. I was so glad I checked, as I always assumed it was the size of a water rail and would have been looking for a much larger bird. It has disproportionately large feet, ideal for its favoured boggy habitat but otherwise it has a similar shape and colouration of a water rail. It astounds me that such a small bird with short stubby wings can be found so far from their normal range and then remain faithful to a particular spot.

On a Monday morning, a friend and I decided to try our luck and, on our arrival, there were more than the normal amount of cars in the car park, a sign we hoped that the bird was still there. The RSPB staff informed us that the crake usually appeared, albeit briefly, in the same patch of sedge in front of the right hand side of the hide. Could we be lucky? When we arrived at the hide there were already about twenty other birders, all crowded at the right hand end. An array of telescopes, cameras and binoculars trained on a rather small area of sedge, close to the hide. Surely our chances were good? Conversations were conducted in hushed tones and, after a while, it became clear that this bird was not going to show easily. Some of the birders were on their second or third visit and still had not seen it. Others had stories of people spending up to eight hours watching without success. Perhaps it would not be that easy after all.

After around an hour with only the occasional movement in the vegetation which briefly raised the heartbeats of those in the hide but turned out to be a young coot or moorhen, I was starting to get restless. We gave it another half an hour and then decided to leave, thinking: I bet the birds pops out directly after we turn our backs.

I did start to question my half-hearted attempt to see a 'lifer'; after all, hardly anyone else had left. Should I have stayed longer, should I go back? Perhaps it had already slipped away and was homeward bound? No perseverance, no patience - that's my problem.

Back home, I received a text from my friend; the crake had made a brief appearance at around 1 pm, that was an hour and half after we left! I told myself that even if I had been there it was no guarantee that I would have seen it. After all, I was told of birders sitting next to one another and one would see it and the other not!

I know that I probably will not have a better chance to see this bird but should I go back? I was not sure.

I did return, two days later. I had dropped my wife off at Lakeside shopping centre and so had a couple of hours to spare. Once again, the right hand end of the hide contained a number of expectant birdwatchers - after all, yesterday the bird had showed again briefly! Evidently the tiny crake had continued to remain faithful to the same small patch of vegetation and all our lenses were trained on the area. One hour passed and still no sign, although my hopes were still high. At this point I think I began to suffer from "birdwatcher's hallucinations" where I started to imagine various obscure bits of dried vegetation or mud as the bird. Then, just as the second hour was about to elapse, someone broke the silence with the words, "there, moving left" but despite everyone focusing on the spot the bird had disappeared. Only one or two lucky birdwatchers saw it! I gave it another fruitless fifteen minutes and then decided it was time to call it a day.

So near and yet so far and this time I did feel disappointed. Once again, I kept thinking: would another hour of patiently watching have brought its reward?

I came to the conclusion that twitching is too stressful for me, even for perhaps a 'once in a lifetime' Baillon's crake!

Protecting My Nuts (Part II)
September 2012

It was a lovely sunny morning and as I stepped outside into the back garden my attention was suddenly grabbed by a sound, a rhythmic, tap, tap - tap, tap - tap, tap - tap, tap. Initially, I thought it was a neighbour engaged in some gentle DIY but then I realised it appeared to be coming from somewhere at the bottom of my garden. Walking slowly forward, the tap, tap – tap, tap, started again and then I remembered what the sound was. Its September, my hazelnuts are not yet ripe but that is definitely the sound of a great spotted woodpecker opening a nut. The operation was being conducted in the pear tree but as yet still out of sight. As I neared I could make out the black and white woodpecker through the branches busily at work extracting his or her meal. Deciding to leave the bird to enjoy the contents of the nut I backed away. Later, I returned to the pear tree and there, about four foot from the ground, in a depression on a rotten part of the trunk was a superbly suitable 'anvil'. Wedged in was a neatly opened, empty, half hazelnut shell. Perhaps I should describe it as a vice rather than an anvil.

On the ground below were a number of empty shells, evidence that this was not the first time this location had been used. This was not the only work bench in use, as later in the week I heard the same noises on a couple of occasions coming from my neighbour's apple tree. The bird, which turned out to be a female was very adept at remaining elusive while plundering my tree as the first indication of a visit was always the tap, tap, tapping. It has been a poor year for the hazelnut crop and almost daily I am now expecting the arrival of a grey squirrel who

I am sure must be able to smell the nuts as I very rarely see them at other times of the year. So, by the time the nuts are ready to fall I think there will be only lean pickings for me.

An empty nutshell

Winter Stores
November 2012

It was not long after I had discarded on to the lawn the rather 'tired' looking peanuts from the bird feeder and refilled it with fresh nuts when a flash of white, pink and dazzling blue landed in the apple tree. It was a handsome jay and with sharp black eyes it surveyed the scene before 'bouncing' down onto the lawn.

I watched through binoculars from the kitchen window as it quickly gulped a number of whole peanuts before flying off. Within twenty minutes the bird returned and this time I counted the number of peanuts it swallowed: sixteen; the last two could still be seen gripped in its partly open bill. I threw out another handful of peanuts and over the next hour the bird made a further five visits, the last two hampered by the bullying tactics of a pair of magpies. Nonetheless, I estimated that this bird, about the same size as a jackdaw and certainly the most colourful of our corvids, collected over sixty peanuts in total! The maximum I counted in a single visit was twenty! I could have sworn that I could see its cheeks and throat bulging with the nuts and subsequent investigation revealed that the bird does in fact have a sublingual pouch in which they store and carry food.

The jay is mainly a bird of woodlands and not a common bird in my garden with usually only one or two sightings annually but this year with the poor acorn crop, their main food source, they have become a frequent visitor to many gardens. No doubt the peanuts have been stashed safely underground - hopefully, to be retrieved in leaner times over the coming winter months.

A Dream Bird
January 2013

It was around two p.m. and I was horizontal on the settee, drifting in that most pleasant zone, between being awake and asleep when I heard my wife call my name, rather quietly, as if not sure whether to disturb me from my siesta. Her next sentence, "there's a flock of birds in the garden and they appear to have crests" quickly brought me to the vertical position. As I left the settee in my wake, my semi-shutdown mind was trying to catch up, asking questions. What size are they? Could it be? How many and what colour? There! My wife pointed to the gingko tree, I looked... they had to be. I reached out for my binoculars, always by the back door. I focussed. They were, unbelievably, waxwings and in my garden! I counted these striking winter visitors from Siberia two or three times before being happy with a total of thirty-five birds. Then, to my amazement, as one, they swooped down towards us and descended on the berries of a guelder rose that was growing in our neighbour's garden but overhanging ours and situated not fifteen feet from us. For a few amazing seconds, half a minute at most, the shrubby tree was alive with flapping wings and acrobatic hungry feeding before, at some unseen signal, they all departed.

I could not help but think that these beautiful birds with their magnificent crests, which I always think gives them a slightly annoyed look, must have been rather desperate. For I have on occasions, over the last couple of months, watched a number of blackbirds, two fieldfares, a song thrush and even a wood pigeon, slowly deplete the juiciest and the most accessible berries. What was left I thought looked rather too shrivelled and meagre to warrant a stopover in our garden.

All said and done, I shouldn't have been totally surprised. Only that morning I had been having a conversation with another local birdwatcher and discussing the fact we had yet to see any waxwings this winter, despite various size flocks having been reported in a number of locations in South East Essex, including some close by.

Even so, I would never have dreamt they would turn up in my garden. All the more remarkable is that this is the second winter running that waxwings have visited my garden, albeit only ten individuals last year.

Aren't Plants Clever?
June 2013

Throughout time plants all over the world have no doubt continuously evolved in order to carve a niche for themselves and, therefore, perpetuate their species on this precious planet. In order to flourish, there appears to be a constant battle taking place between the myriad species of flora for space, sunlight, pollination and nutrients etc.

Yet, one plant in our vegetable plot seems to be taking what I would call a rather casual approach to survival! My wife had sown some salsify plants (Tragopogon porrifolius) of which four had developed and have now grown to a height of approximately four foot, each plant having developed up to ten purple/blue flowers.

One afternoon I noticed that all the flowers had closed. Remarking on this occurrence to my wife, she enlightened me with the fact that goatsbeard (Tragopogon pratensis) is the wild variety of salsify and its old name is 'Jack go to bed at noon'. I had to find out just how accurate the name was and indeed the plants own time-clock. After two or three days of observation I declared to my wife that our flowers were closed at around a quarter past to a half past one; in fact, they were running over an hour late! It was a few days after that it suddenly dawned on me that the plants weren't that late - they were on Greenwich Mean Time and I was using British Summer Time, a much more recent invention!

Somewhat relieved that our plants were behaving correctly it set me thinking as to why and how do they do that? If the plant relies on pollination by insects, why close at midday, losing the mostly warmer afternoon temperatures when more insect pollinators are likely to be on the wing or indeed crawling around? Indeed, not only does it go to bed at noon but on cloudy mornings it appears to be reluctant to get out of bed, with the flowers only a third or half way open dependent on the thickness of the clouds and therefore the levels of light. All in all, the amount of sunlight must further restrict the chances of pollination. Perhaps, as the salsify is more of a Mediterranean plant and therefore would normally enjoy more sunlight, it is less of a problem but what about our local goatsbeard?

Just how do these plants know the time to close their petals? Can they track the sun and know when it reaches its zenith or have they a built in time-clock set to noon? How do they measure the amount of sunlight to decide when to open and by how much - have they a light meter? What are the mechanisms that allow a plant to control the opening and closing of its flowers? Do these plants rely on insect pollination or have they another method? At what time do the plants start to open? (I need to get out of bed early to find the answer to that one!)

So many questions from a birdwatcher! Please if anyone can answer them I would very much like to know.

Meals on Wheels
July 2013

After an early morning drive through Brittany we arrived at the port of St Malo to catch the ferry back to Blighty. While waiting in the queue, I noticed a female house sparrow making a number of quick, short flights from the ground up to the radiator and number plate area of a car parked in an adjacent lane. After a series of sorties, it then flew to the car behind and did the same thing, on occasions hanging on when it could get a grip to probe around the grill. It repeated this behaviour on two further cars in the line before moving out of sight. I can only think that this bird was exploiting the fact that the cars having driven recently through the French countryside and had numerous squashed insects on their fronts. Now that's what I call being resourceful!

Against the Odds
July 2013

My wife and I and a couple of friends had just had an 'all you can eat' breakfast at the Haywain in Fobbing (we only do this once a year, honest!). Feeling that we made too much of the offer of further food we decided a stroll around One Tree Hill would be the answer to our excesses.

The morning was hot and sunny as the recent spell of hot weather continued and as we got out of our cars, Nick Stanley, the Thurrock Ranger, came out of the information centre. He was delighted to inform us that there had been sightings of silver washed fritillary butterflies and white admirals in Northlands Wood and no wonder, as these species had been locally absent or very rare for a number of years and were now frequenting an area that had been coppiced by Nick.

I had never seen either butterfly before and, therefore, I only had a very vague idea what to look for but help was at hand. Another Basildon Natural History Society member who was with Nick came across with his camera and showed us an excellent picture of a silver washed fritillary.

As we walked in the hot sunshine along the edge of the trees we marvelled at the number of marbled whites flitting through the grass and wildflowers in the meadows. This would seem to be another butterfly that has increased locally over the past ten years and, in fact on this day, they appeared to outnumber the meadow browns.

Entering the woods, the air immediately felt fresh and cool; such a contrast to the dry hot conditions outside. As we made our way along the dappled paths is was not long before we had our first sighting of a silver washed fritillary.

Despite having seen a photograph, I was not prepared for the actual size of the butterfly. Surely it must be one of Britain's largest, flying with slow but strong wing-beats, propelling it around swiftly in the patches of sunlight, looking like a large comma. Indeed, we did see a number of commas along the more open paths

On occasions a fritillary would land with wings open allowing through binoculars a view of its beautiful orange and brown intricate markings. When the wings are closed you see how I assume it gets its name, a dusting of silver wiped across the lower part of the hind wing. At times, two or three of these beautiful individuals would be swooping past us as we stood transfixed.

The white admiral proved to be an altogether more elusive butterfly. However, we did eventually catch sight of this faster flying species, mainly black with white barring. When it did briefly alight on some bramble flowers it had its wings closed and then flew off before we had time to study. Despite further searching we did not see another white admiral so decided it was time to go.

As we emerged from the shady woodland the vista out across Stanford-le-Hope and Corringham lay before us. Traffic on the ever busy A13 road rushing by below us and in the not too far distance the vast foundations for Europe's largest container port under construction. What a contrast between nature's world and man's ever increasing footprint.

In addition, having seen some headlines from the recently published the 'State of Nature', an assessment by twenty five of the UK's leading conservation organisations of our wildlife, I had felt somewhat downhearted. It painted a not unexpected but nonetheless gloomy picture of the plight of many of our species including butterflies. Therefore the events of the morning made me realise just how special those moments in a local reserve had been.

P.S. Two days later my wife and I went back, determined to get a better sighting of a white admiral. Luck was with us, as we approached the coppiced area we met Peter Furze and guess what he was watching: yes, a white admiral! As we approached, it flew up but alighted a short distance away and landed with wings wide open allowing us to see its delightful, fresh markings at close range. And of course we once again marvelled at the sight of the silver washed fritillaries.

P.P.S Unbelievably, on the 8th August a single silver washed fritillary was feeding on a buddleia in my garden!!

In Search of a Kingfisher
November 2013

It was probably a month ago, during an innocent conversation with my wife, that I happened to mention a kingfisher. To this she commented that considering it was such a colourful bird she had never seen one apart from on the television. Well, I saw this as a challenge, perhaps a chance for me to impress my wife by tracking and finding one for her to observe in the wild.

The first problem is that kingfishers can be very elusive in winter, moving from location to location depending on food supply and the weather. In saying that, a few nearby places have of late reported sightings of a kingfisher on a number of occasions. So, keeping an eye on the local birdwatching websites I narrowed it down to two areas (lazy I know but I needed to increase the odds -after all my reputation was at stake). Unfortunately, the websites don't always give the exact location – and that was the case with the kingfisher reports. Yes, I do feel guilty, yes, I do want it on a plate!

The more consistent reports were from Langdon Nature Reserve but I knew this could mean any one of a number of ponds/lakes (when does a pond become a lake?). However, the same reports also included tufted ducks which made me think that these small, diving ducks would more likely be on the larger bodies of water and I would therefore be able to exclude the smaller ponds!

So, after a trip to Tesco, we stopped off at the Langdon visitor centre and walked through the woods to the lake. At this point in an effort to lower my wife's expectations I did explain that despite their bright colours they are not that easy to see if they are in shadow and sitting motionless,;they are also quite small, slightly smaller than a starling and, of course, it might have moved on by now.

It was a cold but bright day so I decided we would walk clockwise around the lake keeping the sun mainly to our backs. All around the perimeter were patches of vegetation with branches overhanging the water and in the middle an island with more suitable places for a kingfisher to perch while patiently watching for a small fish passing below.

Every few yards I would stop and scan the water's edge with my binoculars. The tufted ducks were there so I was even more convinced that we were in the right place! By the time we were half way round I was sure that if it was anywhere it would be on the island. After all it was a safe haven with plenty of cover and fishing points.

As we moved round I trained my binoculars on each new part of the island that came into view. Would I be able show my wife a kingfisher?

Nearing the point at which we started and my hopes by now fading, my wife began to feel the cold and the ground was a little muddy and slippery underfoot. I decided go down to the waters edge to scan the last part of the island and then I saw it dart out, a flash of blue and orange as it flew fast and low, and away. Despite my shout of "there it is" my wife was looking elsewhere and missed it. So close!

I tried to persuade my wife to walk back along the bank to see if we could find the bird again but by now, despite gloves, her hands were 'frozen' and we headed back to the car. I took comfort in the fact that I found the right location and I was right about it being on the island and it was the only kingfisher I had seen this year, albeit very briefly.

Still, I will keep watching the websites and no doubt we will be out and about looking for this 'jewel' of the waterside. Perhaps in warmer weather though; after all, an old name for a kingfisher is the 'Halcyon'.

Birds of a Feather
December 2013

.... Flock together. Well they certainly lived up to the saying when we made a visit to Hemsted wood in Kent. Working with directions from other birdwatchers, we parked alongside two or three other cars (always a good sign) and made our way into the wood. The directions were exact: walk approximately two hundred yards along the track and in a clearing is a single oak. This is where the birds had been seen. We found an oak at approximately the right distance and set up our telescopes but somehow it didn't seem right. After a few minutes a dog walker came along and we asked him if other birdwatchers had been here. His answer confirmed our suspicions; there were three similar entrances into the wood and he had seen birdwatchers at one further along the road. Back into the car and once again we parked next to some other cars and started to walk along the track with tall, straight conifers on either side.

After walking around one hundred and fifty yards, we came to the edge of a large clearing and as we stood and surveyed the surrounding tree tops we heard the calls, a series of metallic 'glipp-glipp-glipps'.. Looking round we couldn't see any sign of the birds; then the calls became clearer. A small flock then came over the trees and into view, landing in the tops of the conifers quite close to us. We hurriedly put up our telescopes and, as we suspected, they were crossbills. It got better; at the very tip of one of the conifers, amongst the common crossbills, was one of the birds we had come to see, a magnificent male parrot crossbill!

We had probably been there for only fifteen minutes and already I had seen a species for the first time. As the name suggests, this bird differs from the common by having a much larger, deeper bill and a thicker neck. We watched the flock for a few minutes before they flew, calling as they disappeared back over the trees. Late 2013 has seen an 'eruption' of parrot crossbills from its normal range in Russia and Northern Europe with a good number of birds turning up in parts of Eastern England.

Further into the clearing, we could see another birdwatcher with his telescope at the ready so, as things were quiet, we decided to see if he had seen anything. When we got there, we could see fifty yards in front of him, an oak tree a few light brown, curled leaves still hanging on!! He turned out to be a local birder and explained that this was the tree that the birds frequently returned to. More birders arrived and now there were six of us talking, with telescopes (and two cameras) pointing at the tree. After thirty minutes any conversation abruptly stopped when someone said, "I can hear them". Seconds later, they came across the clearing and swooped down into the tree! The flock was around fifteen in number and were mainly male and female common crossbills but then, after a short while, someone said, "there it is; to the right" and soon I was looking at a beautifully marked male two-barred crossbill, another 'lifer'! It stood out, its brighter red plumage and the two broad white flashes on the wings, it was unmistakable. Crossbills, with their uniquely shaped bills, feed on pine seeds so it was intriguing to see them in an oak tree, some just preening, others apparently probing the areas of loose bark. Then the local birder informed us that the other reason for them choosing this particular tree was that nearby, just out of sight, were two puddles where they often dropped down to drink. Being pine-seed eaters, they evidently need to drink regularly to aid their digestion. On this occasion none took a drink but flew off again calling excitedly.

Things went quiet, so my friend and I decided to have a walk to see what else might be around. We returned to the 'tree' about forty-five minutes later, having been surprised how silent the area was with only a pair of great tits seen in the woods and a flock of around twenty fieldfares flying high overhead calling.

By now, there were eight birdwatchers lined up in front of the tree; some feeding from their lunch-boxes, others chatting over past experiences. It wasn't long before the crossbills, along with the two-barred, came back to the very same tree. We watched these agile birds, the green and yellows of the females and the reds of the males making a colourful scene. Then, to our surprise, another small flock of crossbills flew in and it did not take long for someone to find the parrot crossbill amongst the newcomers. I could not believe it; here was I, watching three species of crossbill in one tree, two of which have travelled far from the vast conifer forests of Northern Europe and Russia! Just to add to the variety, two siskins were also in the same tree. The beauty of it all was that the birds seemed relaxed in this one tree and gave us birdwatchers the rare luxury of time; time to study, compare and admire.

Then, at what seemed a prearranged signal, a number of crossbills dropped down to drink, just as the birder had explained earlier. As we continued to watch them slake their thirst and fly back up to the tree, I could not help but think of that saying, 'birds of a feather flock together' and then I looked along the line of 'birders' in their muted colours.

Essex Man in Spain
February 2014

Day 1

Suitcase and rucksack packed, airline tickets, euros and passport all present and correct. The only thing left to worry about before I embarked on my first birding 'holiday' with four friends in Spain was the weather. The UK, having been hit by a series of storms and periods of heavy rain over the past two months, was due to be battered by yet another storm on the day we were to fly out to Barcelona.

At Southend airport we watched nervously as dark clouds gathered on the horizon but at least the wind remained light. As we boarded the plane a few drops of rain were in the air but we took off on time, relieved and hoping for kinder weather over the next four days.

We were lucky, later that day the storm struck causing damage and chaos in many parts of the UK, including disruption at Southend airport.

At Barcelona, as we crossed the road outside the airport to meet our guide and driver, a single cattle egret flew low overhead: not a bad bird to begin the long weekend. Introductions completed and cases loaded, we set off with Alberto, our guide, driving the mini-bus. It was around 11.30 and the temperature was a balmy 16c as we made our way out of the city under blue skies and bright sunshine, we were immediately struck by the apparent dryness of the terrain, all in complete contrast to the soaked, windswept conditions back home.

As instructed, we were dressed in warm clothing and with tripods and coats in the tops of our cases for easy access, we were ready to begin birdwatching before we had even arrived at our accommodation. Not that we needed coats for at our first stop after an hour or so, at a café for coffee, the temperature was still rising. Just to illustrate this, out of the window we saw a brimstone butterfly patrolling along a flower bed.

Later, as we left the main road and drove on towards the foothills of the Pyrenees, the landscape gradually became more mountainous with the narrow road twisting upwards. Our first birdwatching stop was at Embalse de Santa Ana in a lay-by on a quiet road with towering peaks on all sides. Alberto had chosen this site as it was probably one of the best to see a Bonelli's eagle. We scanned the rock faces and peaks without success until a little later one of our group, further down the road, called out. As we joined him, he pointed to a bird; large enough to be an eagle but difficult to confirm, that was until Alberto immediately identified it as a male Bonelli's eagle, just one of many occasions when his expertise would prove invaluable. It got better as almost immediately the female was located, perched not far from the male; we had time for Alberto to point out the distinguishing features of both birds before the male took to the wing. Then, from nowhere, a peregrine falcon appeared and began to mob the eagle, time and time again diving at him, causing him to take evasive action. Then the larger female flew up to join him and perhaps discourage the peregrine. It appeared to work, the peregrine departed leaving them both to slowly circle in the sky before drifting out of sight. Alberto was even more excited than us because as he explained this was probably the most northerly breeding pair in Spain and we were so lucky to see them!

Driving on we could see buzzards and red kites from the bus, birds that would become a frequent sight on the trip. We then spotted a white stork standing, sentry-like in a roadside field. We wanted to stop and look, as we would on numerous other occasions over the coming days, but Alberto asked us to be patient. Eventually we pulled into a side road adjacent to a field with scattered tall trees. In nearly every tree was an enormous pile of sticks and on top of most of the nests were the occupants, pairs of white storks. We now understood why Alberto did not want to stop earlier. Some were engaged in making a 'clacking' sound with their long, red bills, the sounds echoing across the fields. Others were repeatedly throwing back their heads in a courtship or bonding display. Not that they were the only birds around; we also had marvellous views of an adult male serin, a bird I have only seen twice in my life and then only briefly. Here, I was able to admire the bright yellow on the head, chest and rump and the clean white flanks so boldly streaked. It was here we also saw our first spotless starlings, absent from the UK but, as we were to find out later, widespread here in Spain.

Moving on, we arrived at Mighel de Cinca and parked under a small clump of trees around a disused farm building and from here we had a panoramic view over a wide sandy area with scattered bushes and low outcrops of rock The terrain was teeming with rabbits and this, in turn, attracted avian hunters. It was not long before we saw an immature golden eagle. Unfortunately it saw us and took to its magnificent wings, its white tail with black band showing well. All together in this area we saw three golden eagles and a number of buzzards but unfortunately not the eagle owl which is also occasionally seen here. I had always imagined the golden eagle to be a bird of the mountain tops so it was surprising to see them here at a relatively low level in mainly flat open land but there were an awful lot of rabbits.

Tired but happy, at 6.30 pm, we finally arrived at Lorporzano were we were staying, fourteen hours after getting out of bed. We unpacked, enjoyed a home cooked dinner with, of course, Spanish red wine and were in bed by 10.30, exhausted.

Day 2

Before we came, the organisers had sent each of us a list of birds that can be seen in the area and we were asked which ones we would like to see. We had all ticked wallcreeper and today we were going for it. So, refreshed after a good night's sleep and a hearty breakfast, we climbed aboard the mini-bus at 08.30 full of anticipation for the day ahead.

Once again our route took us back into the mountains to an area called Vadiello. It was not long before Alberto spotted a rock sparrow which most of us managed to see before it flew off, a little further on, the brakes were applied again and we were soon looking at our first alpine accentor (another bird of these rocky hillsides) and, above us, five or six crag martins flying close to the rockface. As we climbed higher, driving through a series of short tunnels carved through the rock, with towering peaks above us and below a twisting river rushing along the valley floor, we were now in wallcreeper country. We manage to park just off the narrow road and fortunately it was virtually deserted; we began to scour the steep, bare red/ orange rockfaces interspersed with stunted trees and vegetation clinging on in cracks and crevices. Then Alberto spotted movement not twenty metres above our heads: it was a wallcreeper! At rest it is mainly grey and black with a long slender down-curved bill. It is only when it moves position and flicks out its broad rounded wings its true beauty is revealed, with flashes of blood red, black and white. To see this elusive, small, delicate bird, not much bigger than a house sparrow (and related to the nuthatches), surviving in this wild harsh environment was indeed a privilege. We continued to watch the bird searching for insects in the crevices, displaying its colourful wings as it moved, before it flew past us and down the mountain, out of sight. While still on the road we could see, high above us, three or four griffon vultures slowly circling and then, joining them, a rare Lammergeier(although in silhouette the distinctive long, wedge shaped tail and long narrow pointed wings were diagnostic). We could not believe our luck, two amazing birds within thirty minutes and both in this beautifully wild landscape. Could birdwatching get any better?

Driving back down to lower levels Alberto had chosen our lunch stop in an area of rough grassland just at the foot of the hills where a private vulture feeding station had been set up. This area provided us with crested larks, a blue rock thrush, black redstart and a dartford warbler. Then our attention quickly shifted from our food to a vulture coming down lower and lower - it was a Lammergeier. Just for a brief moment we saw it on the ground when its huge size became apparent - especially when compared to the five or six swooping red kites who were also attracted to whatever scraps had been left at the station. Then a second Lammergeier came drifting in but did not land; instead, the first one flew up and the two wheeled away together into the distance. We had been extremely lucky to see the pair.

Lunch over, it was once again up to the hills at Salto del Roldan. The single track road snaked up the side of the mountain with eye-watering drops on one side and on the other occasional patches of debris from past rock falls. Everyone was praying we didn't meet anyone coming down! After what seemed an age, we saw a sign up ahead with the words 'precipito' in bold, red lettering, we didn't need telling, but did wonder if it was going to get worse. Eventually, to our relief, the road ended at a small car park where the only other car belonged to a hang-glider who was busy preparing his equipment in readiness for launching himself off the top! As we walked along a narrow, stony path around the side of the hill (I am never sure when a hill becomes a mountain) the views of the valleys, the surrounding hilltops with their rocky outcrops and beyond the open plains, were breathtaking. Then we saw something I don't think any of us had seen before, a griffon vulture flying below us. As we sat on our lofty perch we were treated with fantastic views of the griffons, sometimes above us, sometimes below and some at eye level. Here you could fully appreciate their mastery of the air as they drifted silently past us with just the smallest of adjustments of the tips of their finger-like primaries. At times, a pair would drift effortlessly by, only a few inches separating their wing tips; when one turned, the other instinctively followed, maintaining their distance: it reminded me of the ice-skaters, Torvill and Dean dancing to the Bolero. Alberto decided it was time to move on and somehow the descent didn't seem as scary.

Once again we returned to our base in Lorporzano tired but feeling like a beer to celebrate our amazing day. Our hostess informed us that, as it was the weekend, the village social club was open and gave us directions, a hundred yards up the street, on the right.

The five of us entered and immediately outnumbered the locals, they were playing cards but one got up and went behind the bar to serve us. After ordering a second round we were presented with a plate of Serrano ham and a bowl of peanuts in their shells - a nice touch! We made our way back to enjoy dinner and another early night.

Memory of Spain

Day 3

Today there was no doubt about whether they were mountains or hills: we were going up in the Pyrenees proper, to a ski resort called Astun. It was a long drive and to arrive before it got too busy required us to leave at 07.30. As the road climbed, more and more snow could be seen on the encircling mountains and soon piles began to appear by the roadside. As we pulled into the car park surrounded by beautiful snowy peaks, the sun was just starting to break through the clouds and the temperature was around freezing. Telescopes on shoulders and binoculars around our necks we walked behind a row of hotels and, to my surprise, Alberto pointed out one of the birds we had come specifically to see, it was perched on a hotel roof! Above us was an alpine chough, its yellow bill showing well; and not far away on an adjoining roof was an alpine accentor. I am not sure what the hotel residents made of us with our telescopes trained on the building. We certainly puzzled a few passers-by with one or two stopping to ask what we were looking at and, in a way, we felt relieved to explain. We walked around to the fronts of the hotels, a number with restaurants facing out onto the slopes, looking very much out of place amongst the skiers in their bright multi-coloured clothing and us in our drab greens and browns, with telescopes and not skis on our shoulders! Alberto was scanning the cafés further up on the slopes explaining that snow finches sometimes visit looking for crumbs but, being a Sunday, there was just too many skiers around. We had to give up on seeing any snow finches but we did not waste the crumbs we had specifically brought, we managed to lure down an alpine accentor from a hotel roof and took some great photographs. As we were driving back through the town Alberto spotted a flock of around thirty alpine choughs overhead and quickly pulled over. They gave us a wonderful display of aerobatics and Alberto was able to point out more distinguishing features, as juvenile red billed choughs can also have yellowish bills!

Driving back down out of the mountains we made our way to a wooded valley in the hope of seeing a black woodpecker but without success, so then it was on to San Juan de la Pena and a lunch stop in a wooded area near the monastery. Here we saw crested tit, albeit briefly, and short-toed tree creeper. I was pleased to be informed that all tree creepers in this area were short-toed as I could not discern the difference.

Driving on, we were once again in the foothills of the Pyrenees heading for Sarsamarcuello and an old hilltop castle. Leaving the main road we made our way up and up and up a twisting, rutted, gravel track with once again steep drops to our side. Alberto was oblivious of the fact that we were 'flat' Essex and Kent men not used to such heights and what made us more nervous was that while negotiating hairpin bends he would be pointing out birds to us! This uneasiness culminated in the middle of him doing a three point turn, in order to park at the top, when there was a collective whoa!! as he reversed and we could see no ground from the back window. Gratefully, we climbed out and were soon able to fully appreciate the wonderful views from this lofty vantage point. We walked a short distance to a viewing point and from here we could look across the valley to a massive rock face warmed by the late afternoon sun. Gliding slowly close across the face were five or six griffon vultures, their dark, sharp shadows thrown on to the rock, making it look like twice as many birds were passing. This is what we had come to see; that, and the birds sitting on their nests on inaccessible ledges, still incubating their precious eggs. While watching the vultures our attention was drawn to a series of excited high pitched 'chiaccks' as a flock of thirty to forty choughs (the red billed variety) came past giving us a display of their joyous tumbling and soaring flight while their calls echoed around us. What made the episode so exciting was the fact we were so close and at times the birds were below and then above us. Once again we were reluctant to leave but it was time to go.

Back to base and another visit to the social club to once again discuss the birds and the sights of the day before returning for dinner.

Day 4

Our last day here and it felt colder than previous mornings and surprisingly with even a slight frost. All packed up with only the essentials for birdwatching to hand, we said our goodbyes and posed for a group photograph outside of the converted Bodega where we had been staying.

Our first stop was the cemetery just outside the village. Not all of us had seen a rock sparrow and here Alberto explained was a good place to see them. He was right within fifteen to twenty minutes we found one or two along with several corn buntings. Satisfied, we set off for Ballobar near an area of steppes - dry, mainly flat open plains.

As we approached the steppe area we passed mile after mile of land that had been turned over to intensive agriculture and, as Alberto explained, these once wild areas are slowly being eroded by the expanding requirement for more crops. Irrigation pipelines are being extended ever further and the land is being cleared of stones and rocks but the Conservationists are fighting the plans of the farmers for any further expansion. Let's hope they succeed.

Unfortunately, as we drove on the mist began to get thicker and our hopes of seeing little bustards or indeed any birds started to diminish. By the time we arrived, leaving the main road and driving onto a gravel track, the visibility was down to around a hundred metres at best. As we made our way across the vast open plain, stopping occasionally to peer out into the mist, all was quiet. There was a light breeze getting up which had the effect of sometimes slightly clearing the mist but quite often reducing visibility further. During one such brief spell of lifting mist, we did see a great grey shrike on a low stone wall, our first and only bird of the steppe area so far. We seemed to have covered a good distance and, with the mist enveloping, it heightened the sense of an eerie isolation. How I wished I could see this wild, open place, let alone its special birds. We decided the best course of action was to take an early lunch and hope that the sun would 'burn' off the mist. It was cold and, as we ate our lunch with hats and gloves on, our spirits were low. Then, we weren't just imagining it, the mist had began to retreat and slowly the landscape unfolded before us, bathed in a weak sunshine. Now we were all smiling and soon back driving across the open spaces, the sun getting stronger all the while. The next bird surprised me: it was a beautiful hoopoe, which I had always thought was a woodland bird. It raised its magnificent crest as it flew up on to the top of a low bush, looking surprised to see us. It is in terrain like this with miles of unmarked tracks criss-crossing this mainly featureless open landscape that a guide is invaluable (especially one such as Alberto who knew the most likely sites to yield birds). And so it proved, when after two or three fruitless stops Alberto suddenly braked and told us to keep quiet, in the field up ahead he had spotted a flock of sandgrouse feeding. We quietly disembarked from the bus and, using the cover of some bushes, edged forward; they were pin-tailed sandgrouse and they hadn't seen us. By now we had our telescopes on them and could clearly see the beautiful colours and markings on their wings and back and the slender long tail. Strangely, in the same field just beyond the birds was a fox, lying down and grooming itself in the sunshine while the birds fed. We had the luxury of time to count them, it was estimated that the flock was around one hundred and forty.

Moving on without disturbing their feeding, we soon stopped in an area were the calls of larks seemed to be everywhere. Not for the first time this trip our guide gave us a lesson, this time on how to distinguish between larks. While I just about managed to differentiate between theklas and crested, I did struggle with calandra and lesser short-toed lark. Remarkably, all four were in a small area. While walking around the stony ground in an effort to gain improved views of the larks we put up a stone curlew and, not long after, a short-eared owl.

Having only ever seen stone curlews at a distance, camouflaged against the ground with its streaked brown and white plumage, seeing it at such close quarters (and in flight), I was surprised at how long its wings were and at the amount of black and white on them.

Dotted here and there across the plain were a number of deserted, tumbled down, stone buildings and, almost invariably, a little owl would be in residence, poking its head up as we passed.

Along yet another track, two birds in an adjacent field caught our attention, they were soon identified as black-bellied sandgrouse and on scanning the field we found another four, the black on their bellies showing well. Our list of birds that we had never seen before was growing all the time but time was running out for us to add another speciality of this terrain, a little bustard.

Alberto drove on and eventually stopped to survey the surrounding area when to our left, hidden in the low vegetation, six birds suddenly took to the air and obligingly flew round us and landed a little further away in the same field. They were little bustards, a true icon of the plains and Alberto had found them! We tried to relocate them through our telescopes but, before we could, they once again took to the air and disappeared into the distance. It was smiles and backslapping all round.

But Alberto was not finished yet. After driving for a few minutes he pulled up beside an old quarry and after searching the yellow-orange cliff faces bathed in the warm sunshine we found a striking male blue rock thrush, but this was not the bird we were looking for. We were looking for a handsome bird that we had hoped to see at a number of places over the past days but were always disappointed. Now we had found it and there in our telescopes, we were watching a male black wheatear, its mainly black plumage with pure white on the tail and lower rump, standing out against the bare, sandy quarry face.

Unfortunately, it was now time to leave this amazing haven for wildlife and head for the airport. En route we stopped for a coffee and as we walked to the restaurant spotted a clean, dapper white wagtail, searching for insects at the edge of the car park: our last bird for the trip.

We whiled away the time at the airport finalising our species list for the trip, mine included sixteen birds I had never seen before. They were: Bonelli's eagle, spotless starling, rock sparrow, wallcreeper, Lammergeier, alpine accentor, alpine chough, rock bunting, short-toed treecreeper, thekla lark, calandra lark, lesser short-toed lark, pin-tailed sandgrouse, black-bellied sandgrouse, little bustard and black wheatear. Then, there are those that I had seen before, some albeit only rarely, but were still a delight. They included: golden eagle, serin, chough, raven, crag martin, dartford warbler, hoopoe, griffon vulture, great grey shrike, blue rock thrush, cattle egret, white stork, cirl bunting, woodlark, crested lark and stone curlew. What enhanced most of the birds we had seen on this trip were the dramatic landscapes that provided the backdrop; from the wide, open, desolate plains to the stunning mountains, it gave us the feeling of seeing wild birds in wild places. In saying that, I remember my surprise at seeing an alpine chough and an alpine accentor on of all places a hotel roof top!

We returned to Southend airport late at night and the next morning, still tired, I looked out into the garden, there was a single robin and a wood pigeon, I must admit I did feel a little deflated.

Acknowledgements

To my wife Anne who has encouraged me throughout and 'ironing out' the initial material for grammatical errors. To Ken Laban my knowledgeable companion on many a trip, for his identification skills and many of the photographs in this book. To Mick Gray another friend who also provided photographs. To The Basildon Natural History Society for arranging fields trips and lectures from which I learnt a lot. I would also like to thank Caroline and Leo for making this book happen.

About the Author

Born in 1949 in the East End of London, Bill Goldsmith moved to Stanford- Le-Hope in 1963 then a short hop to Corringham in 1978 where he still lives. Fascinated by wildlife and birds in particular, from a young age, Bill can recall hours spent in his grandfather's pigeon loft which lead to many days wandering Wanstead Flats and some misguided attempts at egg collecting.

Most of his working life was spent at an oil refinery in Coryton until his retirement ten years ago. During this time Bill was able to combine his love of nature with his work and he joined the refinery's environmental department, spending time in the Thames Estuary planning how best to protect that rich environment from oil spills.

Since retiring Bill has much more time to enjoy watching nature. He is a longtime member of the RSPB and the Basildon Natural History Society where he has also contributed many newsletter articles over the years. More recently he has acted as a volunteer for the Essex Wildlife Trust.

Essex Man Goes Wild is Bill's first book. A donation from every sale will go to the Basildon Natural History Society and The Essex Wildlife Trust so they can continue to protect the environment that has inspired his writing.